# THE CURLING LETTERS OF
# THE ZULU WAR

# THE CURLING LETTERS OF THE ZULU WAR

## 'THERE WAS AWFUL SLAUGHTER'

Editors:
Brian Best and Adrian Greaves

LEO COOPER

First published in Great Britain in 2001 by
LEO COOPER
an imprint of
Pen & Sword Books Ltd
47 Church Street
Barnsley
South Yorkshire
S70 2AS

ISBN 0 85052 849 6

A catalogue record for this book
is available from the British Library

Typset in 11/13pt Sabon by
Phoenix Typesetting, Ilkley, West Yorkshire

Printed in the United Kingdom by
CPI UK

# Contents

# Introduction

As the Editor for the Anglo Zulu War Historical Society Journal, I have been truly privileged to have access to the letters of Lieutenant Henry Curling of the Royal Artillery, relating to his experiences in the Anglo Zulu War of 1879.

As is increasingly well known, the British invasion of Zululand began disastrously with the British invaders being met and defeated by the Zulu Army at the battle of Isandlwana.

What is not so well known is that more British officers died in this battle than were lost at the Battle of Waterloo. Of the five who survived, only Lieutenant Curling was at the centre of the front line that experienced the full force of the main Zulu attack. Curling fought his way out through overwhelming numbers of massed Zulu warriors and, miraculously, survived to tell the tale.

At the following Court of Enquiry, his evidence was dismissed as irrelevant, probably because it was too embarrassing to the British military authorities. Curling said little more on the subject – he was after all, a mere Lieutenant. The British commander, Lord Chelmsford, supported by numerous staff officers, had lost over fifteen hundred men and a major battle and, in so doing, humiliated Great Britain. Fortunately Henry Curling consoled himself in his favourite pastime, namely that of writing letters home. In these he paints the most vivid picture of the horror of the Zulu War and, in particular, his account of escaping slaughter at the hands of the Zulus makes for astonishing reading. His letters also allude to the fate of the two Royal Artillery guns that were lost at Isandlwana but, without further details, the exact sequence of events and their final resting place remains unknown even today.

Curling went on to see service in Afghanistan and steadily worked his way up through his Regiment to become a Lieutenant Colonel in Egypt. He then returned to the family home at Ramsgate where he enjoyed his retirement and, as a Justice of the Peace, regularly sat on the bench of Ramsgate Magistrates Court. He never married and it seems that his exploits were unknown beyond his immediate family. He died on 1 January 1910.

Having studied the battlefields of Zululand over many years and written extensively on the subject, I have always been intrigued by this Victorian gentleman who survived the front line at Isandlwana. On a visit to South Africa in March 2000 I had the opportunity of seeing and holding Lieutenant Curling's South African Campaign medal which he proudly wore on a daily basis throughout his remaining military service. On learning that this medal was going to auction, I was able to persuade the owner to allow me to purchase it and so return it to the United Kingdom. Before leaving South Africa, I was honoured to have a meeting with His Excellency Prince Buthelezi, a direct descendant of King Cetshwayo who ruled Zululand at the time of the Zulu War. Prince Buthelezi requested to see Curling's medal before it left Zululand and commented what enormous pleasure it gave him to hold it. I explained to His Excellency that my principal purpose in purchasing the medal was to make it available to members of the Anglo Zulu War Historical Society and the general public at exhibitions.

Within a week of returning to England I received a parcel through the post. The wrapping had disintegrated and it had been resealed by the postal authorities. On emptying the package I discovered that the envelope contained three bundles of original letters written by Lieutenant Curling to his family, including all those written during the Zulu War. Until then I had no idea these still existed. The coincidence of having obtained Curling's medal and received his letters within a matter of days was uncanny. I knew then that I just had to bring them to a much wider audience. Special thanks must go to Wing Commander Jack Curran, a descendant of Henry Curling, and to Tony Lucking for guiding the letters in my direction

## Introduction

A tremendous amount of hard work then followed deciphering and typing the three volumes as well as adding further material explaining the background against which Curling was writing. Brian Best of the Anglo Zulu War Historical Society carefully and diligently carried out this work and I am beholden to him for his dedicated endeavours.

# Foreword

The recent discovery of the Curling letters has given Zulu War historians a fresh insight into a number of aspects of the Zulu War of 1879. Lieutenant Curling, a young Royal Artillery officer, took part in the famous battle of Isandlwana that resulted in a great victory to the Zulus. The British invasion force was virtually annihilated and only a handful of survivors escaped to tell the tale. Curling was one of those survivors – and he was unique because he was also the sole survivor from the British front line that bore the brunt of the ferocious Zulu attack. He witnessed the whole battle and destruction of the British camp and its defenders before escaping on horseback. Curling was very much the family man and a prolific letter writer. His detailed accounts of life in the Victorian British Army make fascinating reading but it is his accounts of the Zululand invasion and Isandlwana that are so gripping.

Curling was a sensitive human being who was deeply affected by what he witnessed at Isandlwana. The publication of this collection of letters constitutes an important contribution to the saga of one of the greatest dramas in British military history, and we have a great debt to Adrian Greaves for his efforts in making these invaluable documents accessible to us.

David Rattray
Fugitives' Drift Lodge
KwaZulu Natal
South Africa

[Reproduction from faded original.]

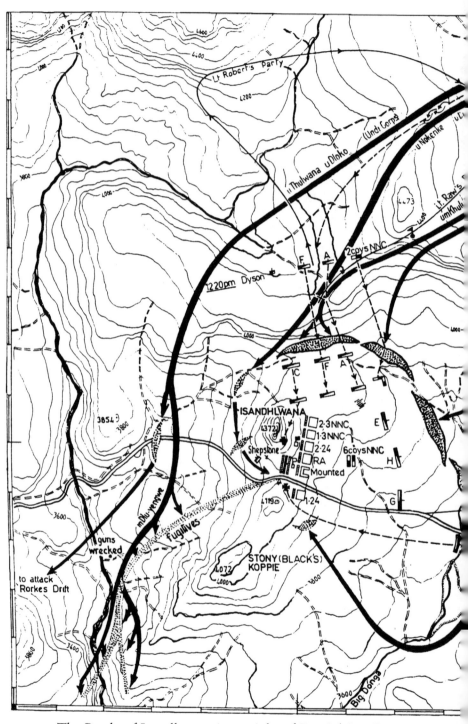

The Battle of Isandlwana (copyright of Dr. Adrian Greaves)

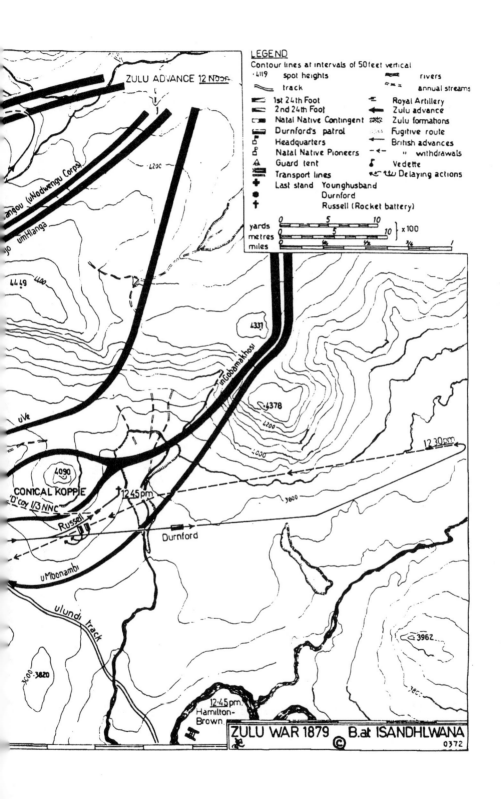

ZULU ADVANCE 12 Noon

ngou (uNodwengu Corps)

umHlanga

4419

4200

4331

ntobamakhosi

4378

4200

4090

12 30pm

CONICAL KOPJE

12.45pm

"D" coy 1/3 NNC

Russell

Durnford

uMbonambi

ulundi track

3820

3962

12·45 pm.
Hamilton-
Brown.

ZULU WAR 1879  B.at ISANDHLWANA

©

0372

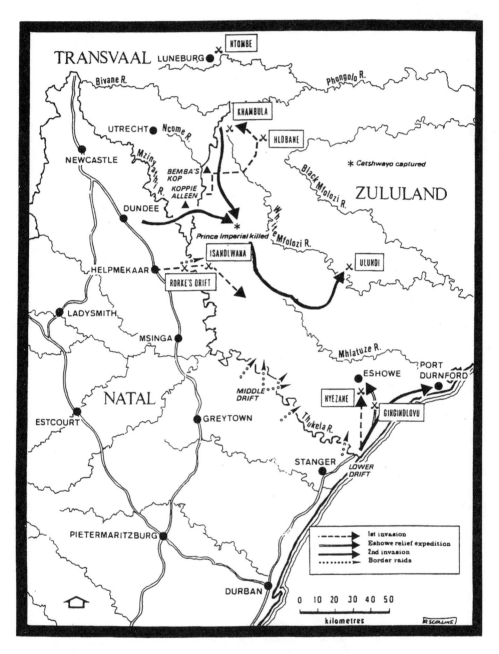

Principal towns, roads and routes together with main actions – 1879.

# Chapter One

# Early Years

On 27 July 1847, Henry and Mary Curling became proud parents of their first-born child, a boy they named Henry Thomas. They had recently moved into a new house in the smart cliff-top area of Ramsgate called St Lawrence. The house was called Augusta Lodge, which was later changed to Chylton Lodge, named after the nearby village of Chilton from where the Curling family originated. It was part of an attractive development designed and built by Edward Pugin, the son of the celebrated architect, August Pugin.[1]

The Curlings were a large land-owning family in the Thanet area of East Kent. One branch of the family became associated with the sea, becoming ships' captains and chandlers. Henry Curling Senior followed a medical career and was a Fellow of the Royal College of Surgeons.[2] Through his contacts as a Medical Officer for the Isle of Thanet Water Company and as a Justice of the Peace, Curling Senior acquired a controlling interest in the privately owned Gas Company that supplied Ramsgate, Broadstairs and Margate with its lighting. It was into this solid and respectable environment that Henry Thomas was born. His arrival was followed by four siblings in quick succession. Alexander was born in 1848 but tragically was drowned in 1861 when he was a pupil at Epsom College. William (Willy) arrived in 1849 to be followed by two girls, Mary Louisa in 1854 and Emily Gutch in 1855.

Mid-Victorian Ramsgate was a small genteel backwater with a busy harbour that was home to a fishing fleet and small shipbuilding yard. By the time Henry Junior had reached his teens, Ramsgate's sandy beach had become a target for the increasing numbers of sea-bathing enthusiasts. Soon there were dozens of bathing machines lining the shore from which emerged strangely garbed hardy souls who braved the cold waters of the English Channel.[3]

The Curlings lived high above the bustle on a cliff-top promenade, which commanded a view over the busy shipping lanes that led to and from the Thames Estuary. As a boy, Henry Junior would have watched the passing ships, mostly rigged for sail, but increasingly steam driven. His pleasant and comfortable childhood was suddenly exchanged for a regime that was both rigid and uncomfortable.

The British upper and middle classes subscribed to that peculiar institution, the Public Boarding School. The aristocracy had long sent their sons to old established schools like Eton, Harrow and Winchester but it was really the mid-Victorian period that saw a proliferation of these establishments. The Industrial Revolution had produced a new wealthy class and the nouveau riche wanted their offspring to emulate the upper crust. Famous schools like Cheltenham, Marlborough, Radley, Wellington, Haileybury, Clifton and Malvern were all established between 1840–1865 and offered a gentleman's education.

Little boys, barely out of the nursery, were packed off to schools that were less concerned with teaching anything academic than ensuring the pupils acquired a proper accent, acceptable manners and a character that was described as 'muscular Christianity'. Greater emphasis was put on sport and religious instruction than on academic excellence and the abiding philosophy was of 'a healthy body, healthy mind'.

The public schools produced the administrators and civil servants for Britain's burgeoning empire. They were also the wellspring of the officer class. Among those schools that produced a large proportion of soldiers was Marlborough, founded in 1843, and it was here that the young Henry Curling was sent to learn how to become a gentleman.[4] Unlike his brother Willy, Henry showed no inclination to follow his father into the medical profession. Furthermore, despite having a strong family connection with the sea, young Henry did not choose the navy as a profession but opted, instead, to go into the army. Like most of his fellow pupils, he missed his family but became conditioned to being apart from his parents and siblings. Maybe this is why he chose to enter the army, another all-male, cloistered environment that would mean long periods away from his loved ones. On entering the Army, a public schoolboy would feel at home, for the values that had been instilled in him would be indistinguishable from those that would greet him in the officers' mess. Young Henry was not one of life's natural warriors. He was sensitive, quiet and modest to the point of being unambitious but he was also mentally and physically tough and was able to withstand the rigours of campaign life better than some of his contemporaries.

This was still the time when commissions in the army were purchased and the wealthier one's family was, the more prestigious the regiment you joined. The Curlings were not a super-rich family so the Guards, the cavalry or a prestigious infantry regiment were not options. The only alternatives were either the Royal Engineers or the Royal Artillery and to enter either, it was necessary to study at the Royal Military Academy at Woolwich. Another consideration was that graduates from the Academy did not have to purchase their commissions and were automatically appointed to the rank of lieutenant. Special classes were offered to those who intended to enter Woolwich or Sandhurst but those who did were regarded, by the more upwardly mobile, as being both idle and stupid for the army was generally regarded as a refuge for the unimaginative and lazy.

Curling would have just turned seventeen when he passed his entrance exam and was accepted into Woolwich. The exams were in two parts. The first, or 'preliminary', tested such subjects as geography, elementary mathematics and geometrical drawing as well as checking whether an applicant could actually read and write. Such was the poor standard of education that as many as a quarter of the applicants failed the spelling test.[5] The second, or 'further', was a gruelling eight-day examination that included a physical test.

It would appear that the examination did not include an eye test, for Henry Curling was very short-sighted. It was not until the 1890s that it was felt necessary to test an applicant's eyesight. In fact, as long as an applicant was a 'gentleman', physical disabilities were overlooked.

The Victorian army had a fair sprinkling of officers who would never have been accepted if they had tried to enlist, even as private soldiers. Garnet Wolseley and Frederick Roberts, who both became Field Marshals, had but two eyes between them. In addition, the latter was only 5ft 2in, well below the accepted height for the Army. Gonville Bromhead, the Rorke's Drift hero, was almost totally deaf, as was General Walter Kitchener, the brother of Lord Kitchener. One-armed officers, like General Sam Brown of belt fame, were rarely retired for reasons of disability. If these were the accepted standards, Henry Curling's short-sightedness would not have been considered a barrier to entering the army.

Having cleared these two hurdles, Curling was accepted as a Royal Artillery cadet where he joined a roll of 270 aspirants. Those pupils who had gained the higher marks were offered places with the Royal Engineers, regarded as the most professional and talented soldiers in the army.[6] Curling would have spent the next two years studying gunnery, drills and horsemanship. He would also have learned that to appear too keen and studious was regarded as 'bad form', so an officer-cadet would emulate the Victorian affectation of disdain for the ambitious swot.

The summer of 1868 saw Henry and his fellow cadets on the vastness of the Woolwich drill ground for their passing out parade. Along with other proud parents, no doubt Curling's family attended, having caught a train from Ramsgate.

On 15 July, Henry Curling was commissioned as a junior lieutenant in the Royal Artillery and posted to the 15th Brigade of Garrison Artillery at Gibraltar. He then began a correspondence with his family, in particular his beloved mother, which continued for the following twelve years that he was on overseas service.

## Notes

1   August Welby Northmore Pugin (1812–1852) did much to revive Gothic architecture in England. Among his most famous work was the interior decoration and sculpture of the Houses of Parliament. His son, Edward, was also an architect but met with less success. His Ramsgate development proved financially ruinous and he was declared bankrupt.
2   Henry Curling (1815–1887) married Mary Ann Warwick Allason (1818–1889) in 1847.

3  Ramsgate was transformed when the London, Chatham and Dover Railway arrived in 1863. It quickly changed from a sleepy backwater to a bustling holiday resort much favoured by Londoners.

4  One of the first pupils who went to Marlborough was Evelyn Wood, who became one of the most celebrated of Victorian soldiers.

5  *For Queen & Country* by Byron Farewell, Allen Lane, 1981, p. 142.

6  John Chard, later to gain fame as the commanding officer at the defence of Rorke's Drift, was a fellow cadet of Curling's. He managed to just scrape into the list of those who were accepted into the Royal Engineers.

# Chapter Two

# First Posting

Before the advent of troop-ships, soldiers were conveyed to their various stations around the world by scheduled passenger ship, which they had to share with ordinary fare-paying passengers. This was a state of affairs that was unpopular with both sides. The army officers usually held a snobbish contempt for civilians while the fare-paying passengers were uneasy sharing a ship with the rough soldiery.

The first letter Curling sent was dated 19 March 1869 from Gibraltar and it offers an insight of what ocean travel was like for those unfortunately obliged to travel by sea, for these were the days before people travelled for pleasure. The *Delta,* a P & O steamer, although clean, was very noisy and draughty. Curling never had a good night's sleep due to the turning of the paddles, the seamen constantly working the sails, the crash of the waves against the portholes, and the noise of the sheep and chickens kept on the deck. The *Delta* also rolled dreadfully and most passengers, including Curling, were seasick for most of the voyage. The ship's officers, on the other hand, considered it to have been one of the smoother journeys.

19th March 1869 Europa, Gibraltar

My Dear Mama,

I have been slow in writing but found it impossible to write on board ship. The screw shook the vessel so much and she rolled

7

so that you would have occasionally to steady yourself with one hand. Will you direct your letters as above as Europa is 2 miles from the town of Gibraltar. I will now begin from when the ship left dock.

The *Delta* is a very long and comparatively narrow ship and consequently rolls very much; in this respect the paddle vessels are far superior, but they are much slower. She is by no means one of the fastest vessels in the P & O Fleet, or the best but, compared with the vessels I have seen before, very comfortable. The cabins look very pretty and are arranged as in the following sketch though I am afraid I have not made it very clear. There are 4 berths in a cabin, 2 on each side, one above the other. I had a (*page torn*) with cotton and found it very comfortable. The partitions are made like ventilators so that there is a regular gale of wind blowing through the berths at night. The berths are very narrow and sometimes the vessel rolled so much that you nearly rolled out of them.[1]

There are only 6 officers and about 70 men in the crew: the bands have been done away with but there is a fiddle which is always played when there is any work to be done by the crew on deck and a harp, so that it in the evenings we had a little music.

There are only 21 First Class passengers on board, 9 of whom were going to Gibraltar. They all came onboard in the (Southampton) Docks and we started very punctually and steamed about a mile down to a buoy where we were moored till the tender came off with the mails. A good many people came off and left by the tender. It was very cold on deck as an East wind was blowing. We lunched while we were waiting for the tender.

We left the buoy a little after three and steamed out to sea. At 4 o'clock the dinner bell went and we all went below. The dinner was pretty good but not much better than onboard the London-Ramsgate boats.

The bread and butter were always excellent. The pilot went ashore off the Needles about 5 o'clock and as we had now got into the Channel we began to roll a great deal. It was very cold and snowed now and then so I went below to my berth. I was not actually ill but was not well enough to eat anything but tea and toast until Tuesday, and generally spent the day in my berth, as it was difficult to walk on deck.

Next morning we were off Ushant (in France) and we pitched rather more. Almost everybody was ill and there were only 7 at dinner on Sunday and Monday. There was no Service on Sunday although we had a clergyman onboard. We went full speed on Sunday and Monday except for a short time on Saturday night when we passed through a snowstorm.

On Tuesday morning the vessel was much steadier and the weather warmer. I felt quite well and enjoyed breakfast very much. Tea and toast is brought into your berth at 7 o'clock, a bell goes for breakfast at 9: it is a hot meal and very good. Lunch of bread and cheese, cold meat etc is at 12.30. Dinner is at 4, tea at 7 and supper at 9. Any amount of beer, claret, sherry etc can be obtained at meals but at no other time. We amused ourselves with playing ship quoits and walking the deck. In the evening, the coast of Spain came in sight and we passed some very fine rocks, the Desertas, I think they called them. The evening was lovely and we had some music. There are very few ladies onboard and they never come out of their cabins. The ports were all shut as soon as we left Southampton and were not opened until we got to Gib, so were almost in the dark. The Mail Steamer was kept beautifully clean quite like a yacht and I should think that in calm weather and when full of passengers, a voyage must be very pleasant.

You cannot imagine what a horrid row there is a nights, the rolling of the ship, the creaking of the screw and the men on deck taking in sail or setting it, together with the water bubbling in the ports and the noises made by the sheep and fowls on deck. I did not sleep at all the first night and very little any of the other nights. The steamer was quite dry, not a drop of water comes on deck but she rolled dreadfully. A gale must be horrible and I don't think I could ever stand a voyage for pleasure in a small vessel.

At meals, the table was divided into little square partitions into which the plates were put to prevent them rolling off the table.

We had a very good passage and the officers said that they

seldom had more than one bad passage in the year. The officers all have cabins on deck, the butcher, baker, cooks, all have shops on deck with their names labelled over them. I talked a good deal to the officers: they live very comfortably but their pay is very small; the Captain only gets about £600 a year and the Second Mate (Uncle Alfred is a 2$^{nd}$ Mate) about £90. On the Indian Station of course they get more. We had 3 passengers for Gibraltar who were going on tour through Spain. One of them was in the Guards, another a chairman of some Indian Railway and I don't know who the other was. The Indian passengers were all either officers, civil service or engineers. The steamer only stopped at Gib 3 hours, as she did not coal.

Most of the officers knew Uncle Alfred. But they had not been on the other line. There were 30 or 40 sheep and any amount of ducks and fowls onboard, as one regiment here gets all its mutton from England.

Monday, 22nd [March]

I will just write a few lines before sending this to the post. The Mail Steamer arrives this evening and the Mail is not made up till then. It is beautifully clear this morning and the mountains covered with snow stand out very clear as well as Ceuta which is just opposite.[2]

In the summertime we are much troubled with mosquitoes, everyone has curtains to their beds. Ants are also a great nuisance and it is said as well as houseflies and centipeedes (I don't know how to spell the word).

We have a boat club and a very good boat, also a first-rate bathing place and library.

They make beautiful carpets here; they are very small and something like Turkey carpets and are I believe expensive. Table covers & rugs are also very pretty.

Give my love to Papa & the Girls & Willie

Believe me, ever

Your affectionate son

Henry Curling

## First Posting

Let me know if you receive this in your next letter as I send it into town by my servant who seems very steady.

He writes of his first impressions of Gibraltar in a letter dated 21 March 1869:

I have nothing to do today and have time to continue my letter. The Bay of Gibraltar is most lovely and looks very well from the deck of the steamer. We anchored more than a mile from the shore and got a little wet in coming ashore as it was blowing rather hard.

On land, we were assailed by a crowd who seized our baggage & quite seemed to deserve the curses they got from the passengers. The carriages here are Irish Outside Cars drawn by mules and are very comfortable and not dear. The town looked and smelled more like an Italian town than any place I have ever been before. The streets were crowded with Moors, Spaniards and soldiers. The Moors all dressed in white and very picturesque.... Some parts of the town are very picturesque with flat roofs and terraces rising above one another up the hill. The people too are dressed very peculiarly and are very dirty and ugly. The regular natives of the Rock who keep the shops are called Scorpions and speak English . . . I then found my captain and went and got my baggage and sent it off to the Europa where my battery is stationed. We walked over shortly afterwards: it is a beautiful walk rather more than 2 miles, the views all the way are most lovely over the bay on to the mountains of Spain which are lofty and much resemble the mountains by the Italian Lakes . . . Our quarters (*at Europa Point*) consist of three cottages built close under the Rock and directly facing the coast of Africa on the other side of the Straits. In the foreground are the quarters of the men and the lighthouse: then the Straits and the coast of Africa which is very grand as the Atlas Mountains are now covered with snow . . . Riding is of course the great amusement. Everybody rides and in fact you cannot leave the rock without a horse as you have to go 2 or 3 miles along the sands before to get into Spain . . . The evenings are very quiet and everything stands out very clear. The Rock is infested with owls. One old fellow lives in a cave about 50 yards behind the cottage and hoots all night long . . . The Colonel of the Brigade is a thoroughly good old fellow: he gives any amount of leave and is very hospitable, always expecting all officers stationed at Europa to lunch with him when they come into town (*Curling hoped to get home on leave in 18 months*) . . . Water is a luxury, it is not laid on to houses but is carried about in casks and cried all over the town. Spaniards drive mules & donkeys about laden with small casks calling 'Agua' . . . All the water here is rain water and is carefully collected into large tanks, it has to be filtered before being drunk.

Curling mentions that his battery had been stationed in Jamaica and had been involved in one of the darker incidents of British colonial rule:

My battery had been stationed in Jamaica during the rebellion. The subaltern in it, Jones, had to execute all the niggers at Morant Bay including Gordon. He says he hung about 60 altogether, the first 3 he had difficulty with as his men had no idea how to hang them and he had to do it with his own hands. He was very fortunate in not having had to sit on Courts Martial as all who did got into trouble.

The Jamaica Rebellion of 1865 began with a minor incident, to which the British authorities overreacted with a display of force and rough justice. When a protest over a small fine was handed down by the magistrate at Morant Bay, the disaffected negro freedmen attacked the courthouse and set it on fire. Governor Eyre, no doubt with the recent Indian Mutiny in mind, sent a naval gunboat and an overland party, including Curling's battery, commanded by Lieutenant Henry Norbert Jones.

The devious Eyre also used the incident to rid himself of a troublesome political opponent, George Gordon. Gordon was a mulatto member of the Jamaican House of Assembly, who constantly agitated for improved conditions for the black population to the point where Eyre had him arrested for sedition. Eyre realized he did not have sufficient evidence to convict Gordon in the capital, Kingston, so he had him taken to Morant Bay, where he could be tried under martial law.

The rebellion was soon put down and dozens were arrested. The courts martial that followed showed scant regard for justice but got full marks for retribution. A total of 177 men and women were hanged, including the unfortunate George Gordon, who was entirely innocent of the Morant Bay disturbances.

When the news reached England, there was a tremendous outcry and debate. For three years there were protest meetings in Hyde Park and Trafalgar Square and furious lobbying to get Eyre and the two naval officers, who presided over the courts martial, brought to book. In the end, they did not stand trial. The outcome, however, was a victory for Victorian humanitarianism and a more enlightened attitude by Britain towards her colonial subjects.[3]

Curling, in common with most Victorian officers, had little contact with his troops and, indeed, rarely mentioned them in his letters. Although he would write a paragraph describing the flora, he used just one line to say, 'The men in the battery seem an awful rough lot but are kept in first rate order.'

Gibraltar was a quiet and comfortable posting that became tedious and restricting. As the months progressed, Curling was hard put to find much to write about. Life had settled into a pleasant round of light duties, picnics and exploring the Spanish countryside on horseback. Curling wrote graphically of his first visit to a bull-fight:

11th June 1869 To Papa

I have been doing a great deal since I last wrote, as latterly I have been riding out into the country several times a week to the different towns and villages, also I have been to the Bull Fight and have rowed a good deal.

The bull fights are the most horrible things I have ever seen. I only went one day and will never go again. They were at Algesciras, a large town on the other side of the Bay about 7 miles off. There are two gunboats here, the Governor went in one of course, and the officers of the garrison in the other.

We had all taken tickets beforehand of course. The Bull Ring is an immense place built of stone and something like a large circus in shape, only much larger and open to the air. The seats are all numbered and divided from each other.

At each of the entrances two dragoons were placed on horse-back just like at the Opera in Paris. There was a State Box in which the Governor sat and opposite to it the Alcalde's (*mayor's*) Box. When the Governor came in the band played 'God Save the Queen'. There were plenty of Spanish ladies present and a few English: the latter all left except two when the first bull came in.

The matadors first came in and ranged themselves all around the ring: They were mounted on horses that would in England be sent to the knackers yard but here the bull ring is substituted. The dresses were very handsome and the matadors (*picadors*) were armed with spears and were well padded and protected with iron. When the door was opened the bull rushed in and immediately charged the matadors one after the other. The spears were no good and the horses awfully gored: some he struck in the chest killing them almost immediately but others were gored in the belly and ran around the ring treading on their own entrails until they dropped dead. It was the most sickening sight I ever saw. Several people could not stand it and had to go out. The first bull killed 4 horses in about 10 minutes. When he got tired of charging them and barbed darts were stuck in his neck to excite him still more: then the swell of the place (*the matador*) came in with a red banner (*cape*) in one hand and a small sword in the other and having received permission to kill the bull, went up to him and holding out the banner, the bull rushed at it and received a thrust from the sword which not being in the right place did not kill him at once as it ought to have done.

The company was not a good one and only one bull was killed at the first thrust. Teams of mules covered in ribbons then came and dragged the dead horses and bull out of the ring and bouquets, gloves, purses and all sorts of things were thrown to the man who killed the bull. Cigars about 2 feet long were also thrown in, typical of the duty on tobacco not having been well collected lately or been reduced. The blood was raked over with sand and another bull brought in. I saw 5 bulls killed and more than 30 horses. In the bull ring at Madrid and other places it is the custom to despatch any horse that has been hopelessly wounded and cannot get up but here they were allowed to roll on the sand in agony until they were dead.

One of the horses that was brought in was recognised as having belonged to an officer in the 28th Regiment who sold it about a month ago as it was utterly used up. It stood two charges from the bull that had been in the ring sometime and, while another bull was being brought in, was bought out of the ring for £6 by an officer named Smith of the same regiment, who has sent it to kennels (*stables?*).

This sickening spectacle did not deter Curling from attending further bullfights. In fact, he became quite an aficionado and he refers to them twice more in his letters. To his mother on 24 July he wrote:

The San Roque bull fights were very good indeed but badly attended. They were by far the best I have ever seen. The matador killed one bull sitting in a chair. He is supposed to be the best in Spain and was certainly very clever.

Curling managed to purchase a horse he named Rufus, on account of his reddish brown coat. Although small, Rufus was very fast and Curling won several races at the Rock's racecourse against bigger opposition. When the hunting season began, Curling rode to hounds along with most of the garrison officers. The Duke of Wellington had introduced fox-hunting into Spain during the Peninsular War and officers were encouraged to participate wherever they were stationed. This was viewed as excellent training particularly for the cavalry and horse artillery. Gibraltar had its own pack of hounds called the Royal Calpe Hunt, and these were frequently augmented by packs belonging to individual regiments.[4]

When Curling sailed to South Africa in 1878, he mentions a fellow passenger '. . . We are taking out a fellow in the Buffs who has with him a lot of foxhounds for a pack his regiment has got in Natal.'

# The Curling Letters of the Zulu War

Curling comes across as a quiet and retiring man, happy to read or write his long rambling letters. He sometimes found his brother officers a little too boisterous and noisy:

> The AAG, Col. Bellairs, has taken up his quarters in a cave near here but is rather annoyed, he says, by bats, insects etc. The Governor is living out here now and his aide-de-camp, Captain Curtis, has the next quarters to mine. He is a very noisy good-natured fellow but keeps so many birds, dogs etc that there is no quiet.

A couple of the Brigade officers who were given extended leave were Captain Webber and Lieutenant Wallace. They made an expedition to South America, where Webber died while crossing the Andes. A fellow subaltern was described as being '. . . a very good fellow but, as he was 8 years in the West Indies he had got West Indies habits and is not very lively. All the officers in the Brigade are very gentlemanly and some of them, Griffin, Reeves and others, are very well off. Griffin keeps 7 horses and 3 or 4 private servants. There are more than 40 horses belonging to officers in the Brigade.'

A new Brigade commander arrived. 'A new General, (*John Jarvis*) Bisset has just come here. His A.D.C, Fitzgeorge, is the son of the Duke of Cambridge and does not seem very bright.'

Curling also had a low opinion of army doctors and frequently referred to them, probably with his father and the newly qualified brother, Willy, in mind '. . . Few of them are gentlemen, they being nearly all Irish or Scotch . . . After 20 years they can retire on £300 a year and they never have any work to do. They become in a short time very inefficient, perfectly unable to take private practice when they retire. For a very stupid and lazy man, it is a good service but a bad thing should they think for anybody else.'

In July one of Curling's colleagues, Lieutenant Archer, suffered an accident.

> A very nice fellow in the Brigade, Archer, was riding through San Roque, a Spanish town about 7 miles from here, when a bee stung his horse and it dashed him against a church: he has been insensible 5 days and still remains so. Of course they cannot

move him so he remains out there but there are always 2 or 3 of us stopping with him.

After a week, Archer was brought back to Gibraltar and Curling gave up his quarters until the injured officer had recovered. The lack of military security at this period is well illustrated in a letter he writes to his mother on 24 July:

> We are hard at work mounting heavy guns but it will take two weeks before we can have any guns to stop Ironclads. As it is at the present, an ironclad might come into the Bay and capture any ships she liked and bombard the town without our being able to do anything to prevent her, as our heaviest guns are only 68 pounders . . . We are mounting several 12 ton guns also but that is interesting and useful work. However, the more work one gets the better though everyone grumbles and the heat makes one fade away to nothing.

The outbreak of the Franco-Prussian War prompted Curling to write '. . . if only they would put us on a war footing and increase the number of batteries, I might gain 100 or more steps towards my captaincy. Besides getting increased pay (£20 a year) at once.'

In a letter dated 29 August Curling wrote:

> . . . I am now living in the town: the Battery was unexpectedly moved in yesterday. I am living in a cottage in the Moorish castle about 400 feet above the sea and in a most windy position: they are called the Look out Quarters on account of their view. There is a nice garden round the cottage filled with fig trees covered with ripe fruit and a summer house stands on the edge of the cliff about 5 yards from the door of my room, from which you can see all along the Rock, up the Straits and the whole coast of Spain, as well as the Neutral Ground and the Mediterranean Sea. There are also no end of mosquitoes of course on account of the garden and I get unpleasant whiffs of cooked oil, garlic etc up from the town; otherwise the quarters are very pleasant.
>
> . . . There is no water to be had up here and the allowance brought up is so small that I have to buy 3d worth every day. On

account of the scarcity of the water, everybody bathes and it is quite curious in the evening to see the fringe of bathers all around the Rock.

The Mediterranean Fleet has now been here sometime: they don't entertain very much. The officers have all, without exception, got short, scrubby beards as a new order allowing them to wear them has just come out: they are obliged to always wear uniform when on shore.[5]

An outbreak of lawlessness across the border was reported to his mother:

17th October 1869

. . . The state of the country lately has been rather alarming. Bands of insurgents have been quite close to Gibraltar. All the Spanish troops have been taken from the Spanish Lines (*border*) to protect the town of San Roque so that there was a good deal of smuggling for a few days. Large numbers of people left all the towns here and are now living on the Rock. At night more than once the country people have come on to the Neutral Ground for safety. Three of us took a long ride on Thursday last to a place about 15 miles from Gib(raltar), hoping to see something, but we saw nothing but a prisoner with his thumbs screwed together, who some soldiers were taking to Algesciras, where he was to be shot. We saw very few people about as everybody has kept indoors or had joined some party.

It is quite safe to ride about in parties as you can always ride away from any unpleasant people as all Spaniards starve their horses, while we feed ours and take care of them. There have been several soldiers shot at close by here and many prisoners shot. Two or three ringleaders have escaped to the Rock where they are now.

The Bay has been full of foreign men of war. We went on board several of them, amongst them, the *Sabine*, an American frigate. The captain was a very nice civil man, not the man you would imagine to hang 6 sailors for mutiny as he did at Cherbourg. There were several attempts at desertion while the

ship was here, and we saw several men working in irons on
board . . .

His long anticipated home leave did not materialize and he became
resigned to waiting another year until he was next eligible. As the most
junior officer, Curling had to perform all the unpopular duties going.
He wrote:

6th August 1870

. . . One new duty is for the officer on duty to visit a guard at the
summit of the Rock after 10 o'clock.
    Now the Rock is 1,400 feet high so you can imagine what it
is like to grope your way in the middle of the night up a mountain of that height. It took me two hours last week. I did not get
back to my quarters until 12.30 and I had to be up the next
morning at 6.30 am. A sergeant with a lantern goes up with you
but it is breakneck work coming down in the dark.

Curling writes in almost all his later letters of his hope in seeing his
family, either with a long leave or persuading his father to take a trip
via Marseilles to Algiers and then Gibraltar. As there are no more
letters from this period, it is not possible to say whether his wishes
came to fruition.
    After two years at Gibraltar, he was transferred to England to help
form a new Field Battery, K/11, at Devonport on 1 February 1871.
This successively evolved, becoming K/16, F/24 and finally N Battery
5th Brigade. Transferring from Garrison to Field Artillery required
retraining as entirely different drills were used. The Field and Horse
Artillery were very similar in that they were both highly mobile,
employing teams of horses to pull the guns and ammunition limbers
to and from firing positions. The function of Field Artillery was to
support infantry with generally heavier calibre cannon, while the
lighter armed Horse Artillery were designed to keep pace with and
fight beside the cavalry.
    In 1859, the Royal Artillery changed the terminology for its for-
mations. A battalion became a brigade; a troop changed to a battery
and the term troop was used for a smaller unit of a battery.

A battery consisted of six guns and a basic unit called a subdivision operated each gun. This consisted of a gun and limber drawn by six horses hitched in pairs to the shafts of the limber. The nearside horses were ridden and the drivers controlled the offside horses with rein and whip. Two gunners sat on seats on the limber while the remaining eight members of the team rode horses. Also attached was the ammunition wagon, which was similarly drawn. Two subdivisions (two guns) made a division, which was commanded by a junior lieutenant. Three divisions made up a complete battery of six guns and were commanded by a captain assisted by a second captain (full lieutenant). The rest of the brigade was made up of artificers, farriers, wheelwrights, harness-makers, saddlers, shoeing-smiths and veterinary surgeons.

## Notes

1   There is some confusion regarding Curling's description of the *Delta*. She was, in fact, a twin-funnelled paddle steamer and not screw-driven. She regularly sailed between Southampton to Alexandria, via Gibraltar and Marseilles. P&O Memorandum 24 June 1896.
2   Ceuta was a Spanish enclave on the North African coast opposite Gibraltar.
3   *Send a Gunboat* by Antony Preston & John Major p. 76–79
4   *The Anglo Zulu War Historical Society Journal (AZWHS)*, December 1998, p. 12.
5   At the request of Queen Victoria, all Royal Navy personnel were required to wear full beards and the Army were to be clean-shaven.

# Chapter Three

# The Ninth Frontier War

During the second half of Queen Victoria's reign, the Army was increasingly called upon to expand and defend Britain's burgeoning Empire. This had to be achieved despite the constraints of tight budgetary limits, a familiar complaint even today, and raising enough men through voluntary enlistment. Compulsory enlistment was never considered until the First World War.

After the Crimean War of 1854–6, Britain had been at peace to the extent that the country had even managed to keep out of the Franco-Prussian War of 1870–1. As a result, the British Army had become complacent and hide-bound, commanded by reactionary officers who saw the service as more of a social club than a serious fighting arm. This was fine for the lazy and unimaginative but by the 1870s a more professional attitude began to emerge as personified by Garnet Wolseley and his disciples.[1]

Unlike the armies of her Continental neighbours, who relied on large numbers of enlisted men to fill the ranks, Britain's Army was made up of volunteers and as a consequence, was numerically smaller.

In contrast, the Royal Navy was the largest and most powerful in the world. This, together with the fact that Britain's foes were primitively armed native armies, gave the illusion that she was as formidable by land as she was by sea.[2] Nevertheless, given her limited resources, the Army had to become adaptable as Britain faced all kinds of enemies in many different environments around the world. Indeed, the British Empire was the most diverse and widespread the world has seen. The Victorian soldiers were called upon to fight such varied opponents as Zulus, Maori, Chinese, Afghans and Arabs. They had to adapt to campaigning in waterless deserts, disease-ridden jungles, rugged mountains and vast plains.

Southern Africa was an area that increasingly involved the British off and on for over thirty years and culminated in the disastrous Anglo-Boer War (1899–1902).

The conflict that started this chain reaction was a minor war that had broken out on the border of Britain's Cape Colony at the southernmost tip of Africa. It was of such little significance that it was barely reported in the newspapers. It was in this far away theatre that Henry Curling gained his first campaign experience. After nine years of serving in a peacetime army and with promotion ever distant, Curling and his Brigade, N/5, were sent to the Transkei as part of the Imperial effort to bolster the Colonial Volunteers in their fight against the warring local tribes.

It was a war where it seemed as if most of the fighting was going on between the Colonial officials and the British Governor, Sir Bartle Frere and his ineffective army commander, General Sir Arthur Cunynghame. During 1877, the Colonial Volunteers subdued the Galeka tribesmen and resented what they saw as Imperial interference. At the beginning of 1878, the area was still in turmoil with the Galekas slipping back over the Bashee River into the Cape Colony and rousing their sister tribe, the Gaikas, to rebellion. Frere decided a sledgehammer approach was needed and requested reinforcements, including an artillery battery.

N Battery, 5th Brigade consisted of 130 all ranks, seventy-three horses and six guns under the command of Colonel Frances Law. His second in command was Major Arthur Harness, a forty-year-old son of a retired general, who was regarded as dedicated and competent rather than an imaginative officer.

The guns used by the Field Artillery were 7-pounders mounted on what were known as 'Kaffrarian' carriages, with 5ft diameter wheels giving a total weight of only 200 pounds. This made them easier to transport over rough ground. 'Rather a queer dwarfed appearance mounted on their long axles, between their tall wheels'.[3]

22

## The Ninth Frontier War

After the Crimean War, the Artillery had been equipped with the newly invented breech-loading guns but they were found to have a design fault and were no more effective than the old muzzle-loaded guns. At a period when the armies of France and Prussia were equipping with breech-loading artillery, the War Office decided to take the retrograde step of re-equipping the Royal Artillery with muzzle-loaders. It was not until after the Zulu War, that an improved breech-loaded gun finally replaced this ancient throwback.

Curling wrote to his father from Woolwich Barracks:

31st December 1877

> . . . I am taking very little and shall not get a gun as it is too expensive and I am not a good shot.[4]
>
> The papers seem to be quite ignorant that any troops are going to the Cape but I suppose the war in Turkey quite takes all the interest in anything else.

The Russo-Turkish War of 1877–8 in the Balkans was of great interest to the British public, involving, as it did, two of the world's most powerful empires. Although not involved, the British Government hoped for a Turkish victory to thwart Russia's ambitions in gaining access to the Mediterranean, either by way of the Aegean Sea or the Bospherous. The public and press, however, generally supported the Russians, especially after the disclosure that Turkish irregulars had slaughtered between 15,000 and 30,000 men, women and children in Bulgaria during the winter of 1877.

In the event, the Turks halted the Russians with great loss of life on both sides. In the treaty that followed, the Great Powers blocked Russian claims to have access to the Mediterranean. Her ambition thwarted, Russia concentrated on expanding her empire to the east, which led to Britain going to war in Afghanistan in 1879–80.

Curling continued: 'We are taking out tailors and shoemakers as they say you cannot get anything made out there.'

The British colonies in South Africa at that time resembled the American West, inhabited by tough settlers, miners, a criminal element that was attracted to a largely lawless frontier, and hostile natives. In the sparsely populated region where Curling and his comrades were being sent, services and comforts were virtually non-existent, so enrolling tailors and cobblers onto the strength was essential.

On 9 January 1978, Curling and his battery set out from Woolwich Barracks. The next day he wrote:

10th January 1878 *Dublin Castle* To Mama

. . . We marched off the Parade at Woolwich at 7am in a snow-storm: it was pitch dark and snowed all the way down to the river. The ship was laying in Long Reach about two miles below Gravesend so it is very fortunate Papa did not go there as it would have been a terrible business getting off the ship.

All the men were present and sober so we had no trouble and got everything squared up in an hour.

We took a Transport Officer down the river with us who had a plan of the mens quarters with him so we were able to take everything off onboard the tug, the men going straight to their messes. We were kept shivering on the pier at Woolwich for an hour in the snow waiting for the tug.

This is a very fine steamer (3,000 tons) and the cabins are very comfortable though not equal to P & O boats. We passed Ramsgate about 6 o'clock outside the Goodwins (*the Goodwin Sands lay off the East Kent coast*). I saw the lights very well and thought I could make out the Granville Road. We had a clear calm night and expect to be in Dartmouth at 12 today, leaving there at noon tomorrow.

We took two special correspondents down with us to Gravesend, one belonged to the Pictorial World, some illustrated paper.

Curling goes on to describe the *Dublin Castle*:

The men are put up in very airy decks but quite dark, lanterns being used all day. The food is food but quite of the steamer kind. We take on the live stock and four more passengers at Dartmouth. Those on board now are few in number and of very indifferent quality.

The steamer is one of those tremendously long ones being rigged with red and black funnels that you often see passing Ramsgate. She is very low in the water so does not roll too much. There are no bulwarks, only rails so it is bitterly cold on deck and I could not sleep last night for the same reason . . .

Passengers are afraid of steamers carrying troops I believe but our men are quite out of sight and no annoyance to anybody. Directly they get on board ship they put on a sea kit of serge with night caps in which they remain always. They parade each morning with bare feet and shirts open for inspection but have nothing to do all day but sleep. They turn out at 6 and lights are out at 9 and they cannot get anything to drink so will be strong and fit by the time we get to the Cape.

Curling displayed the general ignorance the British had about the tribal problems in South Africa. He also was unsure of the South African term for the natives using three different spellings; Kaffirs, Caffirs and Caffres.

They say the Caffirs always break out about Christmas time, principally on account of the weather.

All former insurrections have begun about that time so we are anxious to see the telegrams from the mail arriving at Madeira today.

It was quite usual at this period for the Castle Line, which served South Africa, to call at the small Devon port of Dartmouth, to collect additional passengers. Curling wrote:

11th January 1878 Dartmouth To Papa

As it is not worth while to go ashore this morning, I take the chance of writing once more. We arrived here at noon yesterday and are off at 11 this morning. What a very pretty place Dartmouth is, more like a Swiss lake than anything else. The harbour is so small that there is hardly room for the ship to swing. There are no passengers of consequence on board except Lady Cunynghame, the wife of the general commanding out

there. Miss Glyn the daughter of the colonel commanding on the
Frontier and whom our major is chaperoning is not much good.

Curling quite often commented on the attractiveness or not of women
he met. This particular lady, who he dismissively describes, was
the daughter of Colonel Richard Thomas Glyn, commander of the
1st Battalion 24th (Warwickshire) Regiment, who had been in South
Africa since 1874. The major with the chaperoning duty was Arthur
Harness, a bachelor. For some time, Mrs. Glyn harboured hopes of a
match between Harness and one of her daughters.

13th January 1878 *Dublin Castle* To Mama

I know you expect a long letter so began today. The change in
the weather is quite wonderful from yesterday: there is not a
cloud in the sky and the sun is quite hot. We are just out of
the Bay of Biscay and in comparative smooth water. We had
fine weather in crossing the Bay but there was a heavy swell as
there always is I believe at this time of the year. I have been very
seedy but am much better this afternoon.

Very little has happened onboard: three men have got DT
and there has been one birth. One of the men's wives was not
found out by the Doctor when medically inspected before we
started: she would not have been allowed to start had it been
known. There will be a good rowing for the Doctor who
inspected them at Woolwich. One of our men has got DT when
we went onboard; another man in the same state is a Chinese
general and the third is an officer of the 28th who is going out
as a volunteer.

The passengers are nearly all Storekeepers and a terribly rough
lot: they seem to have plenty of money and keep very much apart
from us. There is a Missionary on board, two Missionary women
and a young woman who is going out to be married to a
Missionary whom she has never seen.

We have been within a mile or two all day of *The Danube*, a
ship that is taking the 90th (Perthshire) Regiment bound for the
same destination: she seems to be passing us slowly but we shall
probably arrive within a day of each other.

We had a service for the troops on deck today; it was rather effective as we have got several men who sing very well and several musical instruments. There is a passenger onboard who is going out as Chaplain to the Bishop of Capetown. We have also got the Colonial Secretary of the Gold Coast and an old Dutchman who owns 200,000 acres in the Transvaal. He is a very nice old fellow and tells us no end about the Cape.

15th January 1878 *Dublin Castle* To Mama

We are about 30 miles from Madeira . . . Yesterday we were knocking about so much that it was impossible to write. I was ill all day long and did not leave my berth. This ship is the worst seaboat I have ever been in. All yesterday the decks were swept with the sea although it was not blowing hard and we rolled so much that it was impossible to sit anywhere without holding on. We only remain in Madeira one hour, just long enough to get a little fruit on board.

The weather is very hot today and stuffy: it has been raining in torrents and blowing in heavy squalls.

Everyone is most anxious to get in before *The Danube* and our men are very useful in setting and getting in the sails. This is only the third voyage the ship has made and she has been unfortunate in making bad passages but I hope this may be a fast one.

16th January 1878 *Dublin Castle* To Mama

As for the next 17 days we don't see land there will be nothing to write about so I start a letter at once and will try to add to it as we go on. We arrived in Madeira about 5 o'clock the night before last but there was such a heavy surf that no boats could come off so we lay at anchor in the Bay all night about a stonethrow from the shore, rocking and pitching tremendously although there was no wind . . .

The next morning a few boats came off but two were upset in trying to come alongside. They brought a lot of bananas and guarvas onboard but neither fruit is worth eating I think.

Curling echoes the average Victorian's suspicion about fruit, especially of the exotic kind:

> We got into smooth water for the first time this morning and have got all the ports open at last. It is very warm indeed, the thermometer in my cabin with all the doors and ports open is 70 degrees. We have not seen the sun for three days as an East wind we have had continuously since we left England makes a thick mist. We left *The Danube* with the 90th Regiment onboard at Madeira: we don't expect to see them today and wonder who will get to the Cape first. The latest telegrams came onboard at Madeira but there was no news of any consequence . . .
>
> Lady Cunynghame turns out to be a very nice old lady but it is a pity we have not a few nice passengers onboard. We got a number of Cape papers at Madeira but they are worse than even the Thanet papers and do nothing but revile each other. One paper makes out that the disturbances are of no consequence, another that the whole colony will soon be in a blaze.

Madeira was the terminal of the southbound cable system at that time. This factor became crucial during the next two years, as London was not in direct communication with the Cape. This contrasted with India that was able to report, on a daily basis to London, the progress of the Afghan War.

The tedious progress of the *Dublin Castle* continues for the next seventeen days down the west coast of Africa.

> We are really in the tropics now: thermometer in my cabin this morning was 87 degrees. . .We have seen no fish but flying fish and porpoises: no sharks or whales. Tomorrow we cross the Line (*Equator*) and hope that in three or four days to see the weather a little cooler . . . There is not much to get out of the passengers. There is one buck on board who always wears gloves even at meals but the majority are the dirtiest looking brutes you ever saw. It is an advantage in one way that you can always get a bath in the morning without any difficulty . . .

## The Ninth Frontier War

3rd Febuary, 1878 Cape Town To Mama

We arrived about 10 this morning and found orders waiting for us. A Captain and Subaltern with one Division are to go to Natal and the remainder of the Battery goes to East London and to King William's Town. I had no choice of going with either party and am going to East London as there is some fighting still going on there. Natal is the best country by far of the two everyone says and the allowances are larger there but at present there seems little chance of any fighting there. We leave tomorrow evening and hope to be done with the sea in about four days. We leave all the women and children here . . .

Curling made a couple of excursions ashore and was not greatly impressed with what he saw:

> . . . Lady Frere sent an invitation asking us to afternoon tea this afternoon but as we are all reduced to flannel shirts and uniform we could not accept it.
> This place is the most dreary burnt up place you ever saw. It looks and smells more like a Spanish town than anything else. There is no pavement and the gutter is the sewer. All the people you meet are different colours and of every nation under the sun. The only good looking men are the Kaffirs who seem very hard-working and steady.
> We drove out to a place called Wynberg this afternoon and dined there. It is a place about 8 miles from Cape Town where all the merchants have their country homes and a great number of invalids from England stay at the hotel there . . .

Sir Henry Bartle Frere (1815–84) was a highly respected and experienced administrator, who had spent most of his career in India. In 1877, he took up his twin appointment as Governor of Cape Colony and High Commissioner for South Africa and resided at the small wine-growing town of Wynberg. His ambition was of a confederation of southern African states under Britain's control, rather on the lines of India. To further this end, he provoked a war against Zululand.

29

Everyone laughs at the war and say that a few hundred policemen could put an end to it but the Exeter Hall people do the harm. As soon as there is any fighting the Caffres send in their women and children to the different missions where they are fed at the expense of the Government . . . The Authorities out here certainly beat anything at home for inefficiency . . .[5]

The following day Curling went out to Constantia to visit the vineyards:

It is a very pretty drive and the people were very civil and gave us tea after showing us around the place. We dined afterwards at Wynberg the same place where we fed on Sunday. They say it is the only good inn in South Africa and they certainly gave us a capital dinner at a very moderate price. The waiting is done entirely by women of every colour from white to ebony. They all wore large crinolines and fringes except for the very woolly heady ones. The Cape wines are very nasty, strong and very rough. I am afraid we shall be reduced to whisky and water as the price of wine and beer is quite prohibitory.

6th February 1878 *Dublin Castle*, Algoa Bay (Port Elizabeth) To Mama

We left Cape Town on Tuesday morning and arrived here at daybreak this morning. We expected to be sent on at once to East London but the steamship people having got away from all authorities are going to remain here for two or three days to get out their cargo. They offer to send us on in a small coasting steamer which is quite out of the question as the men would all live on deck and the weather is so uncertain on this coast that we might be out five or six days.

We are even now anticipating orders to send us on to Natal and hope to find the authorities there who are few in number not so muddled headed as in the Cape Government.

The active service allowances in the higher ranks are very large so every Colonel, Doctor and acting staff officer has gone up to King William's Town and they are not at all anxious for any troops to come up to hasten the termination of the war. Any man with a doctor's certificate can get three guineas a day from the Government besides being found in everything so the ship's doctor has found an invalid who wants to go home to do his duty and is going up to the front with us.

Curling's observation illustrated the casual way the medical service functioned:

We went on shore this morning and drove out to a Caffir location a few miles from the town. They are a dirty miserable looking lot and all quite naked. At the beginning of the disturbances they were deprived of all their guns and assegais.

This is the second town in the Colony and is a miserable place. Provisions are enormous in price, butter you cannot eat 5 & 6s a pound. We lunched at the principal hotel and they charged us 6/6 for a bottle of light claret. The weather is very hot, thermometer this morning was 96 deg. on shore but the houses are built in the same way as in England and it does not seem much hotter than on a still summers day. This seems to be a miserable country to live in: the people themselves say they do not remain longer than their business obliges them.

There has been no rain for nine months here and the country is perfectly burnt up and looks very barren and bleak . . .

Sir Arthur Cunynghame commands out here and everybody agrees that he is a most feeble old gentleman. He has got about 1200 men under his orders and a staff big enough for an army of 60000 men. We have lost all interest in the Russian War (Balkan War): not having any news for four weeks one quite forgets what is going on.

On 10 February Curling and his Brigade landed at East London.

12<sup>th</sup> February 1878 King William's Town To Mama

I never knew what roughing it was until we landed in this dreadful country. The landing at East London is through a heavy surf. We left the ship about 8 in the morning the day after we

31

left Port Elizabeth but finding the water low on the bar had to lay pitching and tossing in a barge for a couple of hours outside.

On crossing we were battened down and quite suffocated with heat as there were about a hundred men with us. Several of them fainted and it was the worst half hour I ever had.

There was so much delay in getting our baggage ashore that it was 10 o'clock at night before we reached our camping ground about 4 miles inland. Fortunately it was a moonlight night so we managed to get our tents up pretty well but we none of us got anything to eat that day from the time we left the ship. Next morning I had to go back to the beach at 5 in the morning to load the heavy baggage.

I got no sleep in the night and thought I never could have got through it but some storekeeper man on the beach gave me something to eat so I got through it. We were hard at work all day loading the baggage into the railway trucks.

On the Monday morning we struck camp at 4.40 to enable us to start by the 6(am) train for this place (King William's Town). It did not matter much as it was blowing and raining all night and we had no sleep. We arrived here yesterday about 10 and are encamped on a sandy plain where the heat is enough to kill you and the clouds of dust prevent you from ever attempting to keep clean. The 24th Regiment gave us a dinner last night and it was the first square meal we have had in this country.

All my kit is smashed to atoms from the constant knocking about it has had. People here go about in anything and eat anything: prices are enormous and if it were not for government rations we could not get on at all.

All the rail up to this place is fortified: Every farmhouse is barricaded & little redoubts are made of railway sleepers. There are pickets of Fingoes, the nigger allies of ours, all over the place and several camps of volunteers near the different stations. Everybody carries arms, the railway people all have revolvers and it is anything but the place for a peaceful man to live in.

I rode out with a party on Sunday afternoon to visit a Dutch lager (sic) about five miles off. It is a large enclosure of wagons and stores into which the cattle are driven at night. In the interior are about a hundred families of people who have left their homes and keep together for safety. On the way up we passed any number of deserted farms. At one station we found some Kaffir prisoners: they are the most awful looking people and one can quite imagine one's fate if taken alive. The news today is very bad, the Kaffirs are in large force about 13 miles from this place and the news is bad all round the country. We expect to be off in two or three days and are quite worked to death. The intense heat makes it much worse as it prevents me from sleeping.

At present we are under orders to march to Queenstown a place about a hundred miles from here.

We have an escort of three companies of the 90th Regt. But it will not be pleasant work as you are never safe from attack from these black devils who murder a man or two and elope. There seems no chance of this being over for another year and we shall be utterly sick of it before then. There is little honour or glory to be got out of it as there are some loafing fellows who sent home flaming accounts of imaginary battles.

I wonder whether the Russian War is quite over. We are quite out of all news.

In all his letters, Curling intersperses his accounts of campaign life with expressions of concern for his parent's health. His father suffered from gout and was concerned about the future of the Gas Company. Curling's mother was a martyr to her teeth and was forever searching for the elusive set that made the perfect fit. Both parents were to become occupied with their other son, Willy's, forthcoming marriage.

In the midst of the squalor and discomfort on campaign, one detects that Curling would have been very happy to return to Ramsgate to be involved in these mundane matters.

26th February 1878 Fort Beaufort To Mama

. . . When we have been there (King William's Town) a few days they sent off two guns to this place with a flying column and last Wednesday I started with two more and another column. We had not had time to get the horses so our guns were taken up by bullocks.

We marched at 5 and in a pouring rain, outspanned for four

33

hours in the middle of the day and camped about 5 in the evening. We did this every day for four days and arrived here on Saturday last. After the first day we had nothing but salt pork and biscuits to eat but in spite of that and getting very little sleep I am in far better health than at Woolwich.

The only thing I cannot manage is the ration meat: it marches with the column, is killed each morning, and is so tough that my poor teeth cannot make any impression on it. The climate of this country is certainly healthy but very unpleasant: it is not hotter than a midsummer day in England but the sun has tremendous power. We attempted to march once in the middle of the day and more than half the men fell out. This is the hottest period of the year and there has been no rain for nine months until a few days ago so of course we come in for the worst. On the four days march up here we passed through only one village as the country is almost entirely occupied by Kaffirs.

We marched as in an enemy's country but these niggers never molest a strong column and only attack small parties. The natives out here are of course quite savage, wear nothing but a blanket and are a murderous looking crew.

Owing to the drought everything here is at famine prices. Meat and poultry are the only cheap things: on the way up I bought two fowls for sixpence and eggs for 4d per dozen. Here we pay 3d a lb for meat & 1s for fowls, 2d each for eggs. There is no butter to be had at any price, potatoes 2d each small ones & no other vegetables at all. It costs 8s a day to feed a horse and they charge at the hotel for board only 9s a day. We are obliged to live there as there is no kit with us and cannot live out of the men's kettles as on the march.

This place in former wars was the central place where a large number of men were kept and there are long lines of ruinous barracks in which our men encamp. We have got here about 500 regular troops, 4 guns and about 500 natives and are expecting orders every day to move off to attack a place about 8 miles from this where a rebellious nigger lives. There is a sort of council sitting every day which I attend as commanding Royal Artillery. If the niggers don't find out the scheme in the meantime I think they will be caught in a net.

We get 4/6d a day extra pay but it won't go very far out here. The country is a very bleak barren looking one, there are no trees at all except in the ravines which are called kloofs and none of the country is cultivated. There are enormous herds of cattle all over the country and a few sheep. There are no roads as we understand the term but only tracks across the country made by constant travelling. Everything is drawn by oxen, the wagons bringing up our stores were drawn by nine span each.

The country is quite unsafe to travel in: everyone is armed and the mail always goes with an escort.

How civilised it looks on the map with towns and villages dotted all over it. The villages consist of one house and the towns of about 20. This is one of the principal towns in the country but it is not as big as Broadstairs.

Of course all European stores are very expensive. Beer 2/3d a bottle, light claret 6/6d and everything in proportion. We get plenty of good grapes cheap and also fair apples. I hope when I write again that we shall have had a tussle with the niggers as it is settled that we move in a few days I think.

A letter from Fort Fordyce dated 12 March is written on notepaper belonging to a fellow officer for it bore an embossed crest with the motto *Finem Respick*:

. . . I am writing now with a camp kettle for a table. We are now quite at the end of the world and up in the clouds. The place is situated on one of the spurs of the mountains to the North of Fort Beaufort and about 20 miles from it. We are perpetually in the clouds and it never ceases raining for more than a few hours at a time. We left Fort Beaufort last Monday week at 10pm in a pouring rain to attack a chief named Tini Macomo. Our road was up a ravine the greater part of the way and as it was pitch dark and raining hard we had constant mishaps. One of my guns went over the side into a stream and in getting it out two of the men went over into the stream as well as myself. It did not much matter as we were all wet through and through before.

After about a 10 mile march we came to the village where Tini lives and halted two or three hours for daylight. We were all so exhausted that we slept on the ground in spite of the rain. At daybreak we surrounded the village but the Kaffirs were too sharp and most of them bolted. We took about 25 of them prisoners and shot down 4 or 5 who resisted. We got all their cattle and burned the village. The remainder of the day and the following one we halted on account of the wet weather making the roads impassable.

The last week we have been constantly on the move driving the Kaffirs out of the valleys taking their cattle and burning villages. It is very poor fun as they never show fight except when they outnumber us 10 to 1. At the same time you cannot leave camp for a hundred yards yourself: one of our fellows was attacked last night while visiting his sentries and had to run for it. We have taken as yet about 1100 head of cattle and the camp is one big slaughter house as they are killed just as anyone fancies them.

It is terrible tough work on two nights we had to sleep out in the open as our baggage could not get up. The days are intensely hot and the nights very cold as a rule although the wet ones are comparatively warm. It seems very hard on the Kaffir women: they are living out in the open with their children and have nothing to eat but there seems to be no other way of taming the savages. They go on fighting even when they know they have not a chance of succeeding. A little of this goes a long way and we are all most anxious to get back to some town. All our little delicacies are gone and we have nothing but our rations, beef, biscuits & tea.

I believe I am to be sent down to King William's Town with my two guns as soon as the business up here is over. I am to get horses in place of bullocks and will probably be sent to Natal afterwards as the Zulus are becoming troublesome and will have to be settled sooner or later.

Even at this early date there was talk of war with the Zulus:

This is rather a murderous business: the few dead Kaffirs I have seen have each had three or four bullets in them: this is not done by one man but by the natives in our pay who are a most villainous lot and very dangerous as they are always firing off their musquets (sic) at anything or nothing and one has a far greater chance of being potted by them than by the Kaffirs. They keep up a running fire all night at anything that comes near the camp and have already shot several of themselves including their Captain.

The heat at Fort Beaufort was intense for several days. The thermometer never went below 93 deg. night or day for the last two days before we left.

This is a miserable country, nothing to be had but preserved things from England. Butter cannot be had at any price: there are no eggs in the towns, the meat is like leather and there are no vegetables but preserved ones from England. Brandy is 8s a bottle so you can imagine the rough way in which we live. I wish you could see us now, black with dirt and our clothes in rags. However it is very healthy work.

We expect to start tomorrow to attack the Waterkloof, a stronghold of the Kaffirs in former wars.

I date this Fort Fordyce but it consists of a mud wall not a sign of a house within 10 miles. In it is a cemetery of soldiers killed in former wars but the tombstones are all being used to make cooking places for the irregulars.

17th March 1878 Fort Fordyce To Mama

We are still up in the clouds and judging by the leisurely way in which things go on am likely to remain here for some time to come.

Yesterday we attacked the Waterkloof or rather went through the form of doing so as there was hardly any resistance. The natives have been told that we would give them their cattle back if they would only come in and give up their arms but as they refused to do so we went in at them yesterday. All night troops were on the move surrounding the valley in which these people live.

We marched at 2 am and got to the top of the mountain path leading down to the valley before daybreak. We then had to lower our guns down with ropes as the road is too steep and

rocky for draughts. In about an hour or two we got all their cattle
but did not get home till dark as we had to drive several parts of
the bush and shell the niggers out of the inaccessible places they
get to when attacked. About 20 of them who resisted were shot
down: I saw three dead bodies in a burning village one in the
middle of the flames. Small detachments of troops are going to
be left all over the country occupying the farm house and I only
hope it may not be my fate to be left here . . . I hope you get my
letters: my last was entrusted to a naked Kaffir who was going
in to Fort Beaufort. Another letter I sent by him to a Tradesman
there never arrived so perhaps yours came to grief too.

The country is very unpleasant in many ways. It's crawling
with snakes, mosquitoes, flies & vermin of every sort. At King
William's Town where we were encamped on stale ground I was
devoured by different animals. Huge beetles 3 inches long used
to crawl over me at night and what with flies and mosquitoes it
was difficult to get any sleep.

General Thesiger has just arrived in the country but we have
not yet seen whether he intends to make any changes in the
arrangements out here. He must be better than the feeble old
man who has been commanding us hitherto.

There now entered into the unfolding drama, its principle actor.
Far from being a charismatic leader, Lieutenant General Frederick
Augustus Thesiger was a pedantic plodder. Although personally
charming and rather reserved, he lacked leadership qualities. He was
unable to stand back and see the whole picture and was inclined to
get bogged down in details that should have been the responsibility
of his staff. His military career showed him to be a conscientious and
diligent officer, perfectly suited to performing staff duties. He steadily
climbed the promotion ladder and became ADC to Queen Victoria
and was made Adjutant General of India. It was during this posting
that he met and became friendly with the Governor of Bombay, Sir
Bartle Frere, a man who would have considerable influence on
Thesiger's life.

When he left India, he was offered the post of Deputy Adjutant
General at Horse Guards but felt obliged to decline. Although he came
from a titled family, Thesiger was not wealthy; he had even married

for love rather than money. Unable to sustain the expensive enter-
taining expected of an officer of his rank, he requested another
overseas posting, preferably India. It was fate that the vacancy he
accepted was as Commander of Imperial Forces in South Africa and
was his first independent command in a career going back for thirty-
four years.

It was also fate that he was able to renew his association with Sir
Bartle Frere, now High Commissioner for South Africa and to share
Frere's vision of a confederation of southern African states under
British control.[6]

> Sir Bartle Frere was living in two barrack rooms at King
> William's Town when we were there and the General lived in
> another so you can imagine the primitive way people have to live
> out here.

Frere spent some seven months sharing the barracks with the officers
of 1/24th Regiment. His presence created friction among the local
colonial administrators, which came to a head when Frere dismissed
the elected Cape Colony Prime Minister, John Molteno.

> We are longing to get back to Beaufort to get a change of clothes.
> Except for washing I have not had mine off for two weeks. We
> always go to bed dressed at night both for comfort and safety. I
> wish our light cavalry could see the light horse here. They are all
> dressed in corduroy and invariably sleep beside their horses with
> their saddles for pillows. In fact the English Regiments are the
> only people who sleep in tents and we have slept out in the open
> several nights. . . I do not anticipate being able to tell you about
> much fighting. You have a very good chance of being murdered
> but none of any open fighting.

Curling wrote to his brother Willy from Fort Fordyce on 25 March:

> . . . We have been now in this place more than three weeks and
> there seems little prospect of our leaving it for some time. We
> came up from Beaufort in what we were told was to be a three
> days patrol and have only the clothes we had when we started.

The weather latterly has been very wet and bitterly cold: at night it is quite impossible to keep warm. I sleep with all my clothing on including the three flannel shirts I brought with me. We don't do anything except make patrols along the ridges of the hills and as all the Caffres have been cleared out there is nothing to do. The niggers never show fight against any number and all the men who have been killed in this war have been murdered whether when alone or when only in twos & threes.

The Natives are very fine men and when in the bush go quite naked with a red blanket over their shoulders which distinguishes them from the tame Caffres who wear clothes. The most extraordinary thing about this outbreak is that most of the Caffres employed in the towns as clerks, workmen and in Government Employment have gone to their tribes and joined their chiefs. Edmund Sandili one of the principal chiefs was a clerk in the bank at King William's Town and has dined with the Governor and other Big Wigs.

Sandili was the old chief of the Gaika tribe. He was described as lame (he had one leg shorter than the other) and alcoholic. By the end of May the war had petered out and Sandili took refuge in a cave. The British were determined to capture him and, knowing he rode a white horse, every captured white horse was checked for a stirrup shorter than the other. He was killed after being badly wounded in a skirmish with Lonsdale's Fingoes.

Sandili had two sons, one of which was named Edmund (Ganga), who had been educated at the Christian Mission at King William's Town and had even visited England. He had worked as a clerk at the Magistrates Office but despite appearing to embrace the white man's lifestyle, he actively egged on his father and eventually joined in the fighting. After his father's death, Edmund and his brother were captured.[7]

Many Caffres are employed as telegraph clerks so they find out beforehand all our movements. There are so few white men in the country that they cannot carry on the work without the help of the niggers.

This is a most beautiful part of the country quite like

Switzerland on a small scale. There are waterfalls and mountains covered with woods and bare & rocky in other parts and the most lovely green valleys. The farmhouses have orange groves around them and are most comfortable in appearance but they are all deserted and most of them burnt down. We have cleared all the Caffres out but it will be some time before it will be safe to live in these parts. We have taken 1300 head of cattle and shot 50 Caffres also have taken about 50 prisoners. The Caffres are looked upon as wild animals and treated as such being shot down on all occasions.

Curling's patronizing and contemptuous attitude towards the black population was typical of the serving soldiers. Paradoxically, the more peaceful natives were less well thought of than the truly warlike. In this protracted campaign in which there were no pitched battles, both ally and foe were equally regarded with contempt.

In the coming war against the Zulus, there was a grudging admiration for the savagery and bravery these warriors displayed in battle. This contrasted with the dismissive attitude the British had towards their own Natal Native Contingent.

We brought out a very good battery mess kit but I got no cooking traps for myself so all my cooking is done in two preserved meat tins. I don't live badly though as we have quite found out the way to cook and always stew the meat for 5 or 6 hours before eating it. I have got a cow we took from the Caffres so we get plenty of milk and we have got any number of sheep we have also captured so we really live very well. . . I am very strong and well and put on about a stone in weight. I don't think you would know me now with two months beard. No one shaves out here and I have not seen a looking glass for the last three weeks.

I only wish we had a little more real work. Imperial troops are quite kept in silver paper out here and they are physically such a poor lot that I don't think they are fit for much else.

Curling was expressing the concern felt by the military establishment about the quality of recruits. The Army Enlistment Act of 1870, one of Edward Cardwell's reforms, had shortened a soldier's active service from twelve to six years with six more on the Reserve. For the first time in its history this gave the Army a large well-trained reserve, and, with a shorter service, had the potential of attracting a better calibre of recruit.

In practice, the physical standard of the average recruit actually fell. In 1870 the average height for a soldier was 5ft 8in but, by the start of the Zulu War, it had dropped to 5ft 4in. Although the number of recruits increased during the 1870s to reach 186,000 by 1879, the British army was still undermanned, with battalions on home duty particularly badly depleted. Most of the recruits came from the lowest rung of society made up of the urban slum dwellers and unemployed farm labourers. Repetitive drilling and harsh discipline welded this unpromising material into a cohesive unit that was steady under fire but bereft of initiative. In fact, initiative was not expected or encouraged; just blind obedience.

The troops that incurred Curling's reservations would have been the men of the 1/24th and the 90th Regiments. By the beginning of the Zulu War, however, these two regiments were considered to be the hardiest in Chelmsford's command, having marched hundreds of miles during 1878. Like Curling, they had become toughened and thrived on the outdoors life.[8]

3rd April 1878 Fort Beaufort To Mama

I think I last wrote from Fort Fordyce which place we left about a week ago and marched round by Balfour and Seymour disarming the natives and leaving small detachments at the principal farms. We did not go more than 10 or 15 miles a day and never started before daybreak as it was very pleasant work more particularly as the country is very pretty and the farms are quite English in appearance. Nearly all the troops with whom we started are left about the country in small detachments and I am expecting orders to take my two guns to the Amatol mountains where the natives are making a stand. Last week they were attacked by Gen. Thesiger and about 5000 men in all but they only killed a few Kaffirs and had ten men killed on our side besides a number who were wounded.

A Captain has come up here and commands over me but I

hope soon to get away from him. I forget whether I told you we had a special correspondent of the *Graphic and Illustrated* with us now: he took a sketch of my guns coming up a path out of the Waterkloof.

The two-page engraving did not appear in the *Illustrated London News* until the following spring, probably to show the difficult conditions encountered by the army during the Zulu War. It was sketched by Melton Prior and shows the gun crew manhandling their gun, which is pulled by a team of oxen. Melton Prior (1845–1910) was the leading special artist/correspondent of his day and his was the original sketch on which this illustration was based. Prior's career spanned twenty-five years, during which time there was only one year in which he was not away reporting. His employers put great demands upon him; as soon as he finished covering the Balkan War he was immediately was sent out with 90th Regiment to report the latest Frontier War. He returned to London by the end of 1878, only to be sent off to Natal when the news of the Isandlwana disaster broke. Prior stayed to report the Zulu War and then the First Boer War of 1880. Small wonder his marriage ended soon after.

Curling continues:

Our camp at Fort Fordyce was full of graves of three men who had been killed in the last war 25 years ago. In digging a trench for refuse in our camp we found the remains of a man who had been in the 2nd Regiment as we found all his buttons and an old fashioned shako.[9]

The great danger out here is being shot by one of the native soldiers. They are firing all day long and are constantly killing one another by accident. We have all had narrow shaves of being knocked over by them. Col. Evelyn Wood who has just come out was received with a volley a few nights ago when going round the outposts. He is a little deaf and did not hear them challenge.

This may be the reason why so few of the Natal Native Contingent was given firearms in the war against the Zulus.

Evelyn Wood (1838–1919) was possibly the most sickly and accident-prone officer to serve in the British army. His career began as a midshipman in the Royal Navy, during which time he fell over-board, and was wounded in the arm in the trenches before Sebastopol. He was only seventeen when he took part in the abortive attack on the Redan, during which he showed remarkable bravery under fire and was recommended for the Victoria Cross. Anxious to see more action, he asked to leave the Navy and, because of his outstanding service and attitude, was given a commission in the Army. He was appointed a cornet in the 13th Light Dragoons and returned to the Crimea. Later, with the outbreak of the Indian Mutiny, he transferred to the 17th Lancers who were being sent to India. It was here that he again displayed great bravery, which was rewarded with the Victoria Cross. During his service in the Crimea, India and Africa he contracted typhoid, pneumonia, dropsy, severe sunstroke, ague, fever, constant intestinal complaints, an ingrown toenail and acute toothache. For a bet, he tried to ride a giraffe, which threw him off and trampled on his face, leaving his nose badly broken and his face scarred. Several riding accidents left him with a cracked neck and a broken ankle. During the many campaigns in which he took part, he suffered from neuralgia, insomnia, swollen glands, eye problems and increasing deafness. At the age of sixty-one he tried to learn to ride a bicycle, lost control and collided with a horse drawing a hansom cab. The horse, understandably, bit Wood on the arm and permanently marked him.

Despite all these mishaps and illnesses, Wood emerged as one of the outstanding officers of the Victorian era and ended his career as a Field Marshal.

Curling continued his letter with an expression of regret:

> I suppose all hope of a European war is now over and more troops will be sent here. There is nothing for them to do now and the niggers never come out in the open and you can do nothing with them in the Bush. They are getting far too many officers out here and we shall soon have more officers than guns. You have no idea what a poverty stricken country this is: no one has any money and all are over head and ears in debt. There is little or no game in the settled part of the colony and a gun is quite useless. There is little chance of these disturbances being over for six months at least as there are 5 or 6000 niggers who

have had their homes burnt and all their cattle taken and who will live now by stealing and murder.

It will be terribly dull here when the disturbances are over and we are not on the move. . . If the Zulus in Natal would only rise we might have some real business. There is every chance of our being sent there soon and there is nothing I should like better than a march of 500 miles.

The reason Curling and his fellow officers were hoping for war was not only for the adventure but that it was the only way to climb the steep promotion ladder. On campaign there were opportunities to do something that would favourably catch the eye of the High Command and enhance promotion prospects.[10]

9th April 1878 Fort Beaufort To Mama

An order has just been received for us to march in an hour or two so I write a few lines before we start. We don't know how long we are to be away or where we are going but think it is a place about 15 miles from this where a chief named Ola is reported to have broken out.

All the villages about the country have been without men for the last three or four days and they are supposed to have gone off to join their chiefs. I went out for a long ride on Sunday and in several villages we saw only 3 or 4 men and hundreds of women and children so they are certain to be up to some mischief now. Except to occupy forts and as guards our troops seem to be little good in this country. They are so slow in moving taking two hours before they are ready to march and they march very badly compared with the natives. In the Bush they are no good at all as the natives can move through it twice as fast being quite naked. The natives live on nothing but the grain they find growing in the fields but our men are quite helpless unless regularly fed with meat, biscuit etc.

There being no biscuits we had flour for two or three days instead and it was quite amusing to see how the men did not know what to do with it. They mixed a little water with it and fried it into nasty tasteless cakes whilst the niggers made ovens in the ground and with a little dripping made very nice bread.

14th April [1878]

I was interrupted in writing to get ready to start but when we were all ready orders came for us to remain where we were so here we are still. I want to get away from this place. The men drink too much and give a good deal of trouble. They buy a cheap kind of spirit for 6d a bottle which stupefies them in a few minutes. A few days ago the two guns we left at Fordyce marched through here on their way to Alice and although they only remained in town 2 hours, when they marched off the men were all dead drunk, so much so that we had to get a cart to lay them in.

Traders were drawn to wherever soldiers were camped and sold the questionable and potent gin known to the troops as 'Cape Mist' or 'Square Face' (after the shape of the bottle). Drunkenness became such a problem during the Zulu War that Chelmsford forbade any trader from approaching the camps.

I have been very seedy the last three or four days with the usual camp illness: this is not a healthy place at all: there are 5 men in hospital with typhoid fever out of 170 troops in the town. This is a large proportion. Two men have died since we have been here from the same complaint. The natives who form the bulk of the population cannot be made to keep any sanitary regulations so with the hot sun one does not wonder at the illness going about.

This climate is only healthy for those who live entirely in the open. I have got a room now and have not nearly the same health as when in the veldt as the open country is called.

It is too hot to go out in the day and it does not suit me remaining in doors all day. When you are living in the open you get under bushes and trees and don't feel the heat so much. People in the country think nothing of sleeping out of doors. In travelling about the country you always sleep in a bullock wagon and if you are mounted you sleep under a bush.

When we were at Fordyce, an old farmer came up with his two daughters to see the camp. They came in a wagon & at night lay down to sleep as a matter of course. This is not at all a pretty country though some of the valleys are lovely. It is very bare and uncultivated and entirely covered with herds of cattle. There are very few white people and thousands of naked savages.

I rode out a few days ago to visit one of our outposts about 6 miles off. The man who was in command said he had not seen a white man except his own men for 10 days. Of course, it is not so bad as this in ordinary times. There is one thing that always strikes me in this country. Every village and town has a very pleasant smell from the orange groves: you can smell them half a mile off.

There was a fight in the main road to King William's Town that we came up by last week and 70 niggers were killed. All their bodies were left to rot by the roadside: no one will ever take the trouble to bury them.

17ᵗʰ April 1878 Fort Beaufort To Mama

At last we have got orders to march. The General arrived here yesterday and orders have just come from him for us to leave tomorrow morning for the Piri Bush in the Amatola Mountains.

I am very glad to be off as there is much trouble in keeping the men in order here and it is not very healthy. I leave 3 men of my small detachment of 30 men behind, sick with camp illness.

The weather is getting cold now, the days are still very hot but out of the sun and during the night it is very cold indeed. I have had a bag made of horse blanketing to sleep in as ordinary blankets are not warm enough. The General says that as soon as this disturbance is over we are to go to the Transvaal but it is not decided yet whether we go by sea to Natal or march through the Free State.

I visited the country yesterday: you would not have thought it had been in existence only 50 years or 60 years as all the gravestones are in a more mouldy and tumbledown state than in an old Churchyard in England. Many soldiers killed in the last war are buried here and there are some handsome monuments to some of the officers killed at that time.

On one stone to the memory of the Sergeant Major of the 7th Dragoon Guards was the following inscription:

> 'Billeted here I am
> Quartered to remain,
> When the last trumpet sounds
> I'll rise and march again'[11]

We don't see much of natives (settlers) as they are too poor to entertain and we have no means of doing so. There is a Ball on Easter Monday and if we are at Alice on that day we may ride up for it as the distance is only 15 miles. Dress in this country is no object: I have not seen a suit of dress clothes yet and all the people in the country wear ready made ones sent out from England. I think you asked me in a former letter what an Assegai is. It is a long light spear with a barbed-head which the natives use as darts. At 20 yards they can make certain of hitting a man. I have got a dozen of them we took from prisoners.

Affairs out here seem to have lost all interest for people at home. They certainly drag on in a very slow and unsatisfactory way. If the colony was only united it could finish the war in a few weeks but they are so much occupied in looking after their own interests that as many Colonists harbour and assist the Caffirs as not.

We are coming under the command of Col. Evelyn Wood who is a very distinguished officer and expect a much rougher time than hitherto.

At this time, Evelyn Wood commanded the 90 Regiment. He was recognized as being one of the outstanding officers of his day and was the only commander to emerge from the Zulu War with his reputation enhanced. Curling would have also been aware that they were both products of Marlborough College, and he frequently expresses a wish to serve under this celebrated old boy:

1. Henry Curling as a young man at the time of the Zulu War.
*(Courtesy of the Anglo Zulu War Historical Society).*
2. Curling in the uniform of a Major, date unknown.
*(Courtesy of the Anglo Zulu War Historical Society).*

3. Drawing from the *Illustrated London News* entitled 'Scene of the Battle of Isandula (sic) with Lord Chelmsford's Advancing Column'.
Note: the guns at 5. are identical to those lost by Curling.

Key: 1. The scene of the conflict. 2. Mounted Infantry. 3. Native Contingent. 4. and 6. Two companies of the 2/24th Regiment. 5. Guns of the Royal Artillery. 7. Company of 24th Regiment under command of Major Black. .

4. Colonel Glyn's force crossing the Buffalo River Valley, near Rorke's Drift, 9 January. Key: 1. Cliff, 200ft high. 2. Waterfall. 3. Lieutenant-Colonel Russell's Mounted Infantry. 4. Major Dartnell's Natal Mounted Police and Volunteers. 5. The 2nd Company, 1st Battalion of 24th Regiment. 6. N Battery, 5th Brigade, Royal Artillery (Lieutenant-Colonel Harness, R.A.).
(From a sketch by Major Francis E White, Paymaster of 24th Regiment)

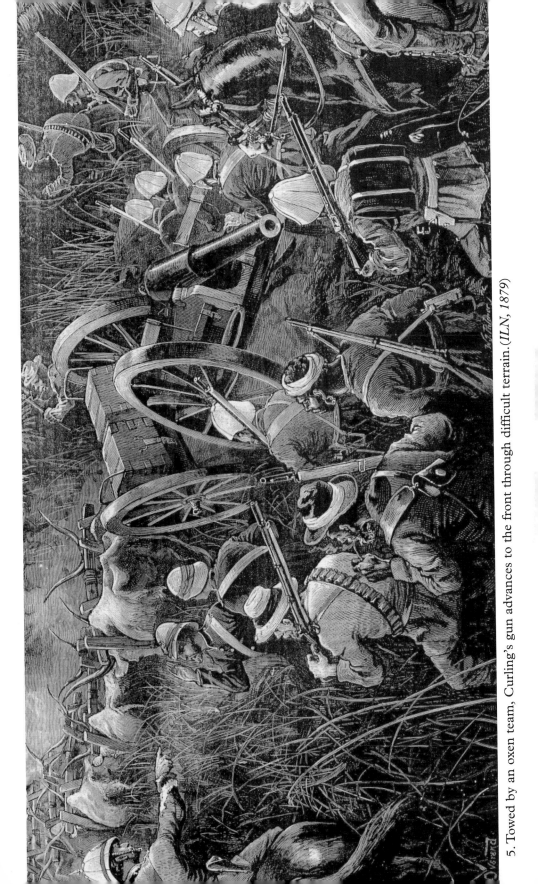

5. Towed by an oxen team, Curling's gun advances to the front through difficult terrain. (*ILN, 1879*)

6. The two guns captured by the Zulus at Isandlwana, and recently recovered.

*(The Graphic, 18*

7. Donga, near Amanzakanzie Kraal, where the guns were discovered. *(The Graphic, 18*

8. & 9. The British Encampment before (above.) and after the Battle (below.)
*(Courtesy of the Anglo Zulu War Historical Society).*

10. The spot where Curling and his guns were overrun. From right, David Rattray, Chelmsford Ntanzi (Warden of the Isandlwana Battlefield), Dr. Adrian Greaves (Co-editor), Bantubezure Ntanzi (whose father fought in the Battle), David Charles (David Rattray's Deputy).

11. The Buffalo River at Fugitives' Drift, where the survivors crossed (from right).

## The Ninth Frontier War

23rd April 1878 Middle Drift To Mama

We left Fort Beaufort the day before yesterday and marched to Alice a pretty little village or rather a town as they call any collection of houses out here. There is a large Wesleyan Mission station here which we went over. It was very amusing to see the Kaffir young ladies sitting down to dinner with napkins and dressed completely from head to foot. As soon as they leave the mission they all eat out of the same pot and wear nothing but a blanket in cold weather. All the biggest ruffians amongst the Caffirs are the school caffirs as they are called: they are well enough educated to be middlebrow. We hoped to have remained at Alice some little time but about 1 am this morning we were roused and told to march in two hours.

There was help for it so we got up at once and came on here. It was a bitterly cold morning and we got nothing to eat before we started as there was no time to get rations. I have a small box of tinned soups so at the first halt we got a good meal. We form part of a force under Col. Wood that is to drive the natives out of the end of the Amatola Mountains. The Kaffirs come out anywhere there are no troops and burn farmhouses: we are sent off at once, of course arriving too late to be of any use. The weather has set in very cold and wintry there was a sharp frost the night before last and not having any winter clothing with us we feel the cold very much. We are only 25 miles from W Town (King William's Town) so if we remain here I shall ride in and get fitted out fresh.

We have quite mastered the science of cooking and live much better out in the veldt than at the hotels where they feed you almost entirely on tinned things from England. Almost all the vegetables are preserved. My cuisine is now in A1 order and consists of a small kettle and a Caffir pot (12 inch gypsy kettle). The latter is most useful as you can bake very well in it and I have some cakes made out of it every morning with the flour they give us in place of bread or biscuit. I have got an iron plate and two tin pannikins and that forms my kit.

When we are together we club our rations and feed together

and as chickens are 6d a piece and milk plentiful we do very well.

By the news we get this morning, war seems almost a certainty.

27th April 1878 Middle Drift.

We are still here although we have been expecting orders to march every day. All the delay prevents any combined movements being of any use as the Caffirs find out everything and get well out of the way. I am still rather seedy and many of the men are so too, a sort of bilious attack with a little fever. Our camp here is in a hollow and, although warm, is not in a healthy situation. There seems little doubt we shall go to the Transvaal as soon as this business is over.

The new General and his staff are mad to get some fighting and are certain to get up some disturbance for the pleasure of putting it down again. Perhaps if a general war breaks out you may see me back with you sooner than we expected as there would be a good chance of our going to Turkey by way of the Suez Canal.

Curling was indulging in some wishful thinking, as the British Government had no intention of becoming embroiled in a Balkan war.

Three days later, on 30 April, the battle of Burns Hill took place. A two-pronged attack was launched on the enemy holding the bush-covered Tutu Ridge. General Thesiger, with the bulk of the force, commanded the thrust from the east, while Colonel Wood completed the pincer movement and approached from the west. For Henry Curling, this was his first opportunity to shine in battle and, unfortunately, he botched it.

Evelyn Wood later recalled:

The Officer commanding the company (90th Regiment) was short sighted, and so unfortunately was the Lieutenant in command of the two guns, and although later several bodies of Kaffirs passed within short range not a shot was fired at them . . .[12]

Unfortunately, of all the many letters Curling wrote, the letter he sent after the battle was lost. It is not clear whether or not it was his failure to open fire that led to his small command being sent to a quiet back-water at Haynes Mill, from where his next letter was sent.

12th May 1878 To Mama

I think I last wrote from Burns Hill. We got rather a sudden order to march to King William's Town and stopping one night at Green Mines got there last Friday week. We got our horses and renewed our kit in a couple of days and then were ordered to march but it was countermanded again and we did not leave until last Friday.

King William's Town is a miserable place and is worse than usual just now as everybody is away at the front and the duties of everyone left consist of sending off things to the outstations, looking after the sick and burying the dead which, as all officers in garrison have to attend when an officer is buried, is a rather fatiguing duty. Unfortunately, two volunteer officers were shot this week. I was there and I came in for both funerals. The last funeral consisted of four men and as they were of different persuasions, they were taken to four different corners of the cemetery and the firing party fired off in the middle – rather a funny arrangement.

The mountains where the fighting is going on are about 12 miles off and we could see the smoke and hear the guns from the barracks. It seems rather funny playing tennis and seeing fighting going on so near. This is a very good tennis ground which is much patronised but I have no fit clothes to wear in Town. It is not worthwhile to unpack your clothes for a few days.

More particularly as you have only a tent to put them in and shaving would only make you look more like a ruffian than ever when you start a beard again. I have got a venerable beard that I am quite proud of. I got a complete kit out of everything and am very comfortable now indeed.

This is a very pretty little place 15 miles from King William's Town and is situated in a narrow valley in the mountains. It reminds me very much of Lauterbrunnen in Switzerland as it is not light until 7 in the morning and is dark at 5 quite an hour earlier than in other places. We are surrounded by a dense bush which is full of Kaffirs so we cannot stir from the camp. Fortunately they have not got rifles: if they had they would make it too hot for us. They have made a breastwork round the camp so beyond night alarms we shall not be troubled.

I am alone with my two guns now and the only other troops here are a company of infantry and a few mounted men. It is the nicest little camp I have been in yet and I hope they will leave me alone for some little time. We have got a charming little mess of 4 members and live very well getting fresh provisions. There is a river of first rate water and a bathing shed, quite the highest piece of civilisation I have seen yet. Our duty consists of keeping guard over the mouth of the valley to prevent any Kaffirs coming in or out. We have outlying picquets all around the camp with a system of signalling to let us know what is going on. I don't see what use my guns are but I want to get my horses in condition before we do any work. I have got now 37 men and 27 horses, a very nice command. I keep a cask of beer in my tent and sell it to the men at 6d a pint, they would pay 2/6d if it were charged. This will get rid of all their money and prevent my having so much trouble with them when we get to town.

Saturday, I rode over to see my Major who is encamped about 10 miles away. We had not met for three months and will probably not meet again for a very long time.

I think I explained that I never had the opportunity of making use of Sir William Coghlan's introduction. Sir Bartle Frere is now 600 miles away from this place and I may never be near him for a long time. Everybody brings out an introduction and I don't see what he can do for me. However, if I ever get a chance I will give it to him.

24th May 1878 Haynes Mill To Mama

We are still here but I am expecting orders to join the headquarters of the battery at a place called Bailey's Grave (not a very cheerful name). My guns have had nothing to do but there has been fighting nearly every day in the mountains by which we are surrounded. The troops go out for three days at a time, returning when their provisions are exhausted. Every night we see the campfires of the Caffres quite close to us in an almost inaccessible mountain at whose foot we are encamped. The day before yesterday they started about 2am to surround it before daylight. The attack commenced as soon as it was light but we could see nothing owing to the dense clouds that always come over the mountains at night but there was a tremendous rattle of musketry so we knew something was going on. Very soon some mounted men were brought in and then two dead ones, all native troops. In about an hour we had 4 dead and 6 wounded men by our tents. There was no doctor to attend them so they lay on the ground all that day and nearly all the next until the troops came back from the bush. We put up a shanty to shelter them from the sun and lent the natives some picks and shovels to bury the dead. Another man died this morning and there is another who has his leg smashed to bits by a bullet but won't allow it to be taken off. The Caffres when attacked had retreated to a place where no one can get at them and completely beat off our people as they surrounded the place – sent for more troops. During the night they managed to make their escape and when the attack began in the morning, the enemy were all gone. There seems no end to this business. More lives are lost now than ever and it seems as if it will last another 6 months. The weather has set in very cold now and we have frosts every night. I don't mind it as I am well supplied with blankets and warm clothing and it suits me better than heat.

After employing unsuitable and ineffective tactics against an elusive enemy, Thesiger finally took the advice of his Colonial officers. In a final and decisive push, each division of his forces were given a specific area to patrol and the freedom to choose when to move. Moving and attacking by night and day, the enemy were finally forced into submission.

There is a delightful bath house on the river and a bathe in the morning is most delicious. We are so near Kings (King William's Town) that we get the papers, provisions and anything we want without any difficulty. I am much annoyed at having to leave this

53

place, more particularly that I lose my nice little command. If any pictures appear about the Caffre war in the Illustrated papers, I hope you will send me a copy. You cannot think what a blessing the papers you send me are. I get them now very regularly and they're everything.

We do not, of course, keep the Queen's birthday in any way except that there is a general attack on the Caffres this afternoon.

I think that when this war is over, if not promoted, I may be able to get leave and be with you next spring. Should there be war with Russia I shall be very fortunate to be here as I should be certain to be promoted soon and sent on to the war and would be eligible for further promotion.

As a subaltern, I can get nothing but a medal. Our Captain, who is only a year senior to me will be made Brevet Major for this little war.

Captain Stuart Smith (1844–79) had, indeed, earned his promotion. The 'Brevet' was a promotion in the field, which was likely to be confirmed at the end of the campaign. It was rather sour grapes on the part of Curling to begrudge his immediate superior his reward, for Smith been mentioned several times in dispatches. On one occasion he had rallied a force that had been ambushed and, by use of covering fire from his guns, he was able extricate the disorganized troops from a perilous situation.

7th June 1878 Bailey's Grave To Mama

. . . I think I last wrote from Haines Mill which place we left last Wednesday week. I am now with the Headquarters of the Battery under Major Harness: I have been away on my own account now since Feb.15th so have no reason to complain. There is a complete lull now, the natives seem to be quite tired of fighting and our people seem to be equally so. The General has gone away to visit the newly annexed land in the Transkei and we do not expect to be moved until he returns.

I only hope they will send us up to Natal where there seems to be a good prospect of some fighting. Unfortunately we are inundated with officers now that have come out with good intent and want something to do so there is a very poor chance of our being sent up country. There are no barracks in the country to put us into so I do not know what they will do with us. The weather has set in bitterly cold and it freezes every night so it is no joke being under canvas.

We always go to bed at 7.30 to keep warm and don't get up until the sun is well up. It is quite hot in the middle of the day the thermometer being between 70 & 80. The men suffer a great deal and there is a great deal of sickness. I have got 7 men in hospital out of 35 in my Division and since we came here three men of the Battery have died of typhoid fever. Quite half my men are ill and only able just to get through their work.

Last Monday we made an expedition to visit the scene of our fight of April 30th, five weeks ago (Burn's Hill). We saw no end of bodies and in one cave where the Caffres had taken refuge at the end of the fight there was quite a pile and we had to step over their bodies to get into it. We found a woman and child that had been killed by a shell and it was quite curious how the trees were cut about by bullets and shells. In this country bodies dry up and do not seem to decay much and there are no vultures or jackalls(sic) to destroy them. The stench one soon gets accustomed to as it is the same as any dead animal.

We have £3 prize money for captured cattle. We all share and share alike from the General downwards so the men get something worth having which they would not get if it was divided in the usual way. If we go to Natal, it will be by sea, I think, as it is almost impossible to get supplies on the road at this time of the year. How fast I am going up the list of subalterns: another year will see me promoted when I look forward to joining you all again.

The Ninth Frontier War was over and another British colony pacified. The war had been an unsatisfactory experience for Curling and his comrades. There had been much discomfort, boredom and precious little action. For months there had been speculation that there could be a war with the Zulu nation and, in his ignorance, Curling was thrilled by the prospect of fighting a pitched battle rather than the hit and run affairs that had marked the recent war.

Notes

1  Garnet Joseph Wolseley (1833–1913) was the most brilliant and successful Army commander of the Victorian era. He gained a reputation for careful planning, preparation and innovation. He soon began to attract like-minded officers who were dubbed the 'Wolseley Gang', by those who were excluded. Among the chosen ones were men like Evelyn Wood, Redvers Buller, Bindon Blood and Baker Russell, all of whom acquitted themselves well during the Zulu War.

2  It was the early reverses during the Anglo-Boer War of 1899–1902 that first showed how vulnerable the British Army had become when faced with modern weapons.

3  *The Story of the Zulu War* by Major Ashe & Captain E. V. Wyatt Edgell, Sampson Low, London, 1880, pp. 187–8.

4  Because of his shortsightedness, Henry Curling was reluctant to purchase a gun. Officers were required to purchase their own side arms up until 1914, when they received standard issue revolvers.

5  Exeter Hall was the South African equivalent of London's Missionary Hall.

6  *AZWHS*, December 1997, p. 21.

7  Proceedings of the United Service Institution of India 1879 Vol. Vlll, *The Kaffir War* by Major M. Gossett.

8  *AZWHS*, December 1997, p. 1.

9  The 2nd (The Queen's Royal) Regiment took part in the fighting during the Eighth Frontier War.

10  *AZWHS*, December 1997, p. 1.

11  The 7th (The Princess Royal's) Regiment of Dragoon Guards fought in the 1846–7 Frontier War.

12  *From Midshipman to Field Marshal* by Evelyn Wood, Methuen & Co, 1906.

# Chapter Four

# The March to Natal

It had been mooted that the Army would be transported by sea to Durban but it was finally decided that the overland route would be the cheaper and less problematical. This entailed a march of some 500 miles through rugged terrain during which thirty-seven rivers had to be crossed. Those who undertook this gruelling march found it stood them in good stead for the coming Zulu campaign.

Major Harness decided not to distribute new clothing, which had been due on 1 April as:

> I think it is far better that they should patch up their old things than wear their good ones for only the Kaffirs to see. Consequently they are kept together by old bits of cloth and very often bits of sheepskin.[1]

Curling wrote:

25th June 1878 Kei Road to Mama

> I think this will be the last letter you will have from me for the next six weeks or two months. We are on our way to Natal by land and this will probably be the last place that any letters can be sent from. There are so many difficulties about transport that

we may travel so slowly that letters may be sent back. The order arrived for us to go to Natal on Monday and we started the following day halting three days at Haines Mill to complete our equipment from K W Town. Since that we came to this place by easy marches and have halted here for a day for the Commissariat people to join us.

The force consists of the 90th Regt. The whole of our Battery and about 100 mounted infantry and is commanded by Col. Wood. We march right through the country occupied by the tribes we have been fighting and are to attack another tribe, the Pondos, if they don't make submission before we reach them.

There are no roads and no supplies to be got on the way so we shall barely do 10 miles a day. There is no fuel to be got the greater part of the way so we shall have to use dry cording and have all provided ourselves with bellows as it only smoulders. We are now in the middle of winter and it is most bitterly cold at night – always freezing. I put on all the clothing I have going to bed and even then cannot keep warm. The men suffer a good deal and the more so that many of them have got fever. I hope their health will improve when we move about and get away from the old camp grounds. The hospital in Kings is full of typhoid fever cases sent in from the different camps: 3 of our men have died from it and there are two or three more that are not expected to recover.

We have more than 10 per cent of our men behind in hospital and have sent home to England 5.

The 90th Regt. have lost by death 20 men and leave 100 behind sick. I have had a touch of fever but am quite rid of it now. Will you address in future to PeterMaritzburg (sic) Natal.

I suppose it is quite certain that there will be no European war: such numbers of officers are coming out here in search of fighting that they cannot think there is to be anything of the kind in Europe. We have got six officers in my battery now, 2 of them senior to me and there are several other gunners awaiting employment so I have no chance of getting an independent command again now. It is a pity we did not get more fighting in the

Waterkloof as I had a good opportunity then of getting mentioned.

There is a picture in the Illustrated (London) News of one of the fights there with my guns in the left of the picture but it is much exaggerated as regards the fighting.

Col. Wood who commands the column is the most energetic, plucky man I ever met, in fact his energy almost amounts to a mania as he wears himself out and everybody under him. He is so plucky that he imagines that everyone is like him and would lead us into trouble if there was any serious fighting.

There are so many difficulties regarding a march to Natal that it is quite possible it may not come off after all.

30th June 1878 Galena To Mama

This place is on the road to Natal about 10 miles from a place called Butterworth you will find marked on the map. Although you see towns and villages marked on maps, they are quite imaginary and for the most part consist of a mission house and a few Caffre huts. This place rejoices in one house of two rooms which is called a hotel and store. They sell bottled beer at 3/6 a bottle and everything else in proportion. We have been on the trek now for a week and have only done 75 miles of our journey. There is a post from Theka two days march from this and after that you will not hear from me for two months or more. I do not expect to get another letter or paper from you unless we are caught up in Theka.

Yesterday we crossed a big river, the Kei. It is about ½ mile wide and 3 or 4 feet deep so you can understand it took us all day to cross. 2 or 3 wagons upset in the water: we consider ourselves fortunate in not losing anything but, as we cross 37 rivers of different kinds before we get to Natal, we are pretty certain to get our traps wet sooner or later. We always start now before daylight and last night did not get the tents up until 10 o'clock. It was a very cold night, nearly freezing, so you can understand it is no joke.

It does not get light now until 7 o'clock and it is quite dark at 5 o'clock but we have passed the shortest day.

In fact just four weeks elapsed before Curling was able to continue sending news of his column's progress:

29th July 1878 Kokstadt

Dear Mama,

This will be the first place we have come to where there is a regular mail since we left Cape Colony.

You will find it marked Adam Kok's Lager (sic) on the map and it is about 2/3rd of the way to Pietermaritzberg Natal. There are only about a dozen houses but after a month in the wilderness it seems quite a large town. We have been on the march now six weeks and have only come 300 miles but it is over mountainous country uninhabited except by savages and we had to make roads as we went along.

With exception of a few Mission stations we have not seen a house for 200 miles and the country being completely bare of wood you can hardly imagine how desolate it seems. We carry provisions for the whole journey with us as nothing but cattle can be obtained on the way and our column takes up 4 or 5 miles of road as we have 50 wagons drawn each by either 16 or 18 oxen. We live very well as we brought plenty of wine spirits as we were not much restricted in baggage.

The harder work we have is in crossing the rivers as the fords are always bad and stony. It took more than a day to cross the St. John's, the last big river we passed.

At the Mission station (Umtata) where we halted on a Sunday we found a real live Bishop and a brand new Cathedral. (A cross was sent out from England). The only big thing about it being the Bell which was enormous and was hung on a gallows outside the Church. One of our men died that day so he was buried by the Bishop, who seemed quite glad to have something to do. He has only about 30 white people in his diocese so does not often get the opportunity of burying anybody.

Our men are still sickly and have not got over the fever that seems to belong to the Country. If they get ill on the march there is very little chance for them as there is no place to leave them at and sleeping on the ground at night and being jolted in an ambulance all day soon puts an end to them. The weather is very trying too: it freezes hard every night (quite an inch of ice in the buckets) and the sun burns you up in the daytime. By putting on all your clothes and an unlimited number of blankets it is just possible to keep warm at nights and I suppose we shall get accustomed to the climate in time.

Major Buller joined us yesterday with about 200 Cavalry so we are about 1000 strong – quite an army for this country.

Redvers Buller (1839–1908), like Evelyn Wood, was one of the 'Wolseley Gang' and regarded as being destined for higher command. He proved to be a courageous and inspirational commander of irregular cavalry during the Zulu War and was awarded the Victoria Cross for several acts of bravery during the British defeat at Hlobane. He had travelled to South Africa with General Thesiger and been handed what could have been a poisoned chalice – the command of the Frontier Light Horse. They were an unruly bunch made up of army deserters, sailors, barflies and border toughs, but by a mixture of example, encouragement and hard discipline, Buller moulded this unlikely rabble into a cohesive and effective force. At this time, Buller's appearance was of a tall, wiry and grim-faced man who was physically tireless, unlike the bloated man he became just twenty years later when he timidly commanded the Army in South Africa at the start of the Boer War.[2]

Arthur Harness's first impressions of the volunteers were less than complimentary. He wrote, 'We do not look forward to their joining us; they are undisciplined and preserve little system in camp, so that the river water wherever we camp, which is very precious, will hardly be kept free from their touch anywhere. The 90th are bad enough, but the volunteers will be far worse.'[3]

Curling continued:

We have been marching latterly through Pondoland, the inhabitants of which country are supposed not to be friendly and have been quite expecting to have a brush with them but there seems no chance of it at present. One night the whole country all around the camp for miles was in flames but whether it had been accidentally set on fire or not we do not know. We were up all night and only kept the fire down with trouble. All the grass in winter is dry and burnt up and the slightest thing sets it on fire. We have gone a whole day over a perfectly black plain without a blade of grass. The worst part of the journey is over now and we are arriving in the borders of civilisation again at last.

3rd August 1878 Kokstadt To Mama

We still remain here but expect to move on Monday and hope to arrive in Petermaritzberg (sic) in ten days or two weeks. We got a telegram yesterday telling us we are not to go beyond Petermaritzberg (sic) for the present, the 90th Regt. with Col. Wood going on to Utrecht alone. This is good news as we shall probably not be sent to the Transvaal and at the same time, if there is any fighting, shall be certain to come in for it and be with the General instead of Col. Wood. We have had so much marching that a few weeks quiet in a town will be a pleasant change. I have not seen my baggage since we left Woolwich and quite expect to find everything in a most ruinous state. We have been waiting here until an ultimatum was sent to the Amapondos asking them to give up the mouth of the St. John's River. An answer is to arrive today and is quite expected to be a favourable one. Should it not be so we are to march on Monday and take possession of it anyhow – we are certain to move at once. The weather has been bitterly cold the last week, we had snow and sleet continuously and the mountains are white with snow. The water in the tent and one's sponges are frozen hard every morning. We are 4000 feet above the sea so the cold is not to be wondered at. At the same time, this is the healthiest place we have yet been at I think: the air is so bracing you feel you could walk forever. There are plenty of buck in the mountain and we are out all day after them.

I am a very poor shot and have not touched one yet.

We hear that two more regiments are on their way out to Natal: should this be the case, we are certain to have a fight with the Zulus as the Government would never go to such expense without something to show for it.

At that time, few British regiments were stationed in South Africa and their companies were scattered over a wide area from the Cape to the Transvaal. They were the 2/3rd East Kent, 1/13th Somerset Light Infantry, 80th Staffordshire Volunteers and 88th Connaught Rangers. When it became apparent that war with the Zulus was inevitable, the 2/24th (2nd Warwickshire) Regiment was sent from their Cape posting to join their sister battalion the 1/24th, in Natal. This was a most unusual event and went quite against the spirit of the Cardwell Reform, which intended that if one battalion was serving abroad, the other would remain in Britain on home duty. Two more regiments arrived by the end of 1878, 2/4th The King's Own, who did not take an active part in the invasion, and 99th The Duke of Edinburgh's Regiment.

'. . .The General expects to be able to finish the war and get home by Christmas so perhaps some of us may be able to get leave then.'

History has shown that commanders who make this boast invariably end up fighting a long hard war. Similar predictions were made about such murderous conflicts including the Crimean War and the First World War.

> Anyway, I am pretty certain to be promoted by next June and must come home on my way to any station except Mauritius, and it would be wonderfully bad luck to be sent there. (*Presumably because of its peaceful isolation*)
>
> All the chiefs of the different tribes whose country we have passed through have been in camp to pay their respects at each halting place. They generally bring a bullock for a present and receive a bottle or two of rum in exchange. They often give us a war dance and it is very amusing as they go through the whole performance of a fight and being all stark naked it is very ludicrous. At one place we saw a wedding feast.
>
> The women had a dance and prepared themselves for it by stripping off their blankets, the only clothing they wear except a few beads.
>
> Should we have to go down to the mouth of the St. John's River we are to take no baggage at all but only enough grain for a week or two. It will be bitter work sleeping in the open without tents but I suppose as the Colonists do it, we shall be able to do so too. There is a force of Irregular Cavalry here commanded by

Major Buller, with Captain Barton of the Guards as second in command. They both have over £6,000 a year but are quite content to rough it out here.

Captain Robert Johnston Barton (1849–79) of the Coldstream Guards served as Buller's second in command of the Frontier Light Horse. During the confusion of the fight on Hlobane Mountain on 28 March 1879, an ambiguous and misleading message from Buller sent Barton and a company of the Frontier Light Horse to their deaths as they rode straight into an advancing Zulu impi.

'Since we have been here we have given a series of dinner parties. The guests have to bring their own plate, knife, fork etc & a box to sit upon and we provide the grub which is very good as our servants are becoming A1 cooks. We always have soup, an entrée, joint, game and a pudding quite as well cooked as in a house in England.'

Curling's cheerfulness had evaporated by the time he wrote to his brother, Willy:

15th August 1878 Kokstadt

We have been nearly three weeks at this outlandish place and are hoping for orders to move to Natal. Unfortunately, as there seems little prospect of a Zulu war, we may remain here some time or be sent to the mouth of the St. John's River to take possession of it.

There seems little prospect of any fighting and indeed there are so many hawks (special service officers) out here that there is little chance of gaining any more credit. I must get a medal now and being only a sub cannot have a brevet, besides I have no chance of any independent command now which is the only way to get on.[4]

We have been more than six months under canvas with only three weeks in barracks and one gets rather tired of the discomfort.

The climate of this place is particularly trying: one's sponge is frozen hard as a brick every night and the sun burns you up in the daytime. I have been laid up last week with rheumatism in the hip and have been unable to walk at all: it is the first attack I have had so must not complain. The cold is knocking our horses up too and they are looking worse than they ever did after the hardest day's march.

Col. Wood at the present time has gone down into Pondoland to see if the chief will give up the mouth of the St. John's without fighting for it. Should he do so we may get on to Natal but there seems every chance of the Niggers behaving in the usual way and not giving in until forced to do so.

Everything in the stores is sold and we have eaten all the supplies we bought with us so we are living now on hard fare, beef and biscuit and tea, which is all very well but is poor stuff when living in idleness.

The only good thing about this place is the shooting and so many fellows are out every day that there is little game left with 8 or 10 miles. When we first came here there were buck in all the hills and the river covered with duck and I even killed three in one day. Should we go into Pondoland, we shall get very good shooting indeed but I trust it will not come off.

Our camp swarms with vultures attracted, I suppose, by the dead bullocks and camp refuse. Some of them are enormous brutes and they come within a few yards of you as they are seldom shot at. The General and the special service officers will do all they can to coax a fight out of the Pondos as having gone to great expense in getting troops out, they will look foolish if nothing comes of it. Pondoland being independent is quite devoid of roads so we shall have to make them as we go along and are certain to have some very rough living. They are the most uncivilised savages we have seen, quite different from the Gaikas and Galekas, the people we have been fighting.

1$^{st}$ September 1878 Umlaas River To Papa

. . . You ask whether we have better maps of the country out here than at home: there are no maps of the country at all. Those printed in England are entirely imaginary and are probably compiled from books of travel. Several times on the march to this place we found that the rivers marked on the map had not existed and we always had to send on the day before to

65

find out whether water was certain to be found at the halting places.

The lack of accurate maps was a handicap during the invasion of Zululand and great reliance was placed on the colonial scouts to seek out the best routes. The Royal Engineers took the opportunity to survey and produce the first accurate maps of the region.

The half-expected fight with the Pondo tribe did not materialize, and the column continued its slow march into Natal.

Notes

1 *Invasion of Zululand* by Sonia Clark, Brenthurst Press, 1979, p. 39.
2 *AZWHS* December 2000 p. 31.
3 *Invasion of Zululand*, ibid, p. 40.
4 A brevet was a temporary field promotion, without pay, given for distinguished conduct and was usually later confirmed. It was not, however, bestowed on lieutenants or subalterns. His medal is now in the possession of the Anglo Zulu War Historical Society.

# Chapter Five

# Preparing for War

After two months of fairly leisurely marching, Wood's column finally reached their destination, the garrison town of Pietermaritzburg. This was to be Curling's home for the next four weeks as Lord Chelmsford (General Thesiger succeeded to the title in October) built up his forces and laid plans to invade Zululand.

5th September 1878 Petermaritzburg (sic) To Papa

We marched into this place on Monday: it is by far the nicest town we have seen in this country and looks far more like an English town than anything else.

The town is full of troops so we are under canvas outside and consequently uncomfortable, as we have to be well-dressed and make the same appearances as if we were in barracks. This colony seems to be far in advance of Cape Colony in every way. People live in far greater comfort and are far more civilised than at King William's Town & Beaufort.

The stores have given way to regular shops that would do credit to places like Plymouth and Exeter in England. There is a capital club where we generally dine as the Buff's (1/3rd Regt) mess is overcrowded, being the only mess here. The General arrived yesterday and inspects us tomorrow. Sir Bartle Frere is expected soon and should he come, I will be careful to present Sir William Coghlan's letter. Everybody that comes here seems to have a letter to him and how he is to pay attention to all of them I don't know.

Nothing is known as to the probability of a Zulu War. There is a large force collected out here now and it does not seem likely they will send them away without doing anything.

(Letters of introduction from some prominent citizen were frequently used to try and gain some advantage or favour for young officers).

This raises another possible reason why Britain went to war with the Zulus. The expensive concentration of a large force had to be justified. A similar situation arose in 1854 when the British and French sent their armies to support the Turks against the Russians. Soon after they arrived in Bulgaria, the Turks defeated the invading Russians and the war was over. Unable to return unbloodied, the British and French decided to land on the Crimean peninsular, some 350 miles away, and destroy the Russian naval port of Sebastopol. This led to the costly and disastrous Crimean War.

Curling continues:

We all have shaved off our beards before marching into town so I cannot send you a photo of an old campaigner . . . there seems little chance of my getting home before promotion and it will require all the interest to be obtained to get a field battery at home. Out of sight, out of mind and we are certainly are at the end of the world here.

Further letters from home are dominated by Willy's forthcoming marriage to Lizzie Ann, and Henry responds with generosity and affection:

8th September 1878 Petermaritzburg to Mama

. . . You cannot tell how much pleased I was to hear about Willy: it was a great surprise and a very pleasant one indeed. I enclose a small cheque for £10 and hope it will not arrive too late.

## Preparing for War

We are living here in great discomfort and hope if we remain under canvas to be sent away up country again. Everybody rides and it rather strikes me at seeing 60 or 70 ladies riding at the Band. However, they are rough specimens and would be keeping farmhouses in England. At Richmond, a village about 20 miles from this town that we passed through on our way here, they gave us a Ball. Some of the girls were rather pretty but they could not dance well and were very colonial.

Curling's patronizing view of the colonials was to land him in trouble the following year. He typically was expressing what most Imperial officers felt towards the locals, and the colonial volunteers in particular, and there was very little fraternization between the two cultures.

We were rather amused by a native servant coming into the room stark naked and dropping wax from the candle all over the floor. This is a very pretty place and seemed to us, who had been in the desert so long, like a City. Everything is very dear, dinner claret 5/- a bottle, beer 1/6 and other things in proportion.

The ladies here are very well turned out and are a peg above Margate jetty.

Should a war break out with the Zulus, there will be a great loss of life on our side as they are undoubtedly 20 times as numerous as the Kaffirs we have been fighting and are well armed.

Curling was not the only one to prophesy a war that would result in heavy casualties. The special correspondent of the *Illustrated London News*, Melton Prior, had just returned to his London office and told his editor, 'You take my word for it, if we do have a war with the Zulus, the first news we shall get will be that of a disaster'.[1]

Curling continues:

. . . I am still living in a tent and have little prospect of getting out of it. We have been more than 7 months out here and have been, with the exception of about two weeks, under canvas the whole time. The climate is quite tropical and quite different from Kokstadt which is only 130 miles distant. The sun in the middle of the day is intensely hot and if we remain any time we are certain to breed fever.

There are two bishops here, though what they do no one understands. Bishop Colenso is one of them, I hope to hear him next Sunday.

In our largely secular society, it is difficult to imagine that the Church wielded such a strong influence over the daily lives of the Victorians. Church leaders were powerful men and if one of them held strong or controversial views, they became celebrities. One such man was John William Colenso (1814–83), the Bishop of Natal.

He was a Cornishman, the son of a mining agent who lost all his money in a disastrous tin mine investment. Brought up in great poverty, the studious young Colenso managed to get into Cambridge on merit and graduate with honours. He had been brought up as a dissenter but realized that to advance his beliefs, he should remain in the Church of England. Overcoming crippling debts, he began to be recognized as an exceptional cleric. When the Bishop of Capetown met Colenso, he was impressed enough to offer him the newly created diocese of Natal. Once appointed Bishop of Natal, Colenso began to upset the traditionalists by questioning some of the literal interpretations of the Bible. He was even put on trial in Capetown for erroneous teaching but managed to survive with his reputation enhanced. He had become newsworthy and Colenso's name became well known in Britain.

Colenso liked the Zulus and they respected him. He was sufficiently interested in them to embark on a remarkable project of producing a Zulu language dictionary, which is still in use today.

Controversy still dogged him and he became something of a tourist attraction, so that visitors, like Henry Curling, would attend his services in the hope of hearing something shocking. Disappointingly, as Curling was to discover, Colenso's sermons were long, complicated and delivered in a rapid high-pitched voice, with his script held close to his eyes.[2]

*Preparing for War*

10<sup>th</sup> September 1878 Petermaritzburg To Mama

You will get this I suppose just after the wedding and hope it may find you quite well and not knocked up by the excitement and fatigue.

It is a pretty little town but we are beginning to get tired of it, or rather we live in such discomfort that we wish to get in the country where we need not keep up appearances but can go about in anything. The sun is getting very powerful now, the thermometer was 97 in my tent today and clouds of dust are always blowing so you can understand white shirts, collars etc are rather in the way.

We have no regular places for meals, too, as every other day, my commanding officer insists on my staying all day in camp, anything but a pleasant duty. I am longing for promotion. For the first six months out here, I was alone and enjoyed it very much but now I have nothing but the meanest duties to do and never being away for a single day makes it terribly monotonous.

Curling was now aged thirty-one and had been a subaltern for ten years. He was experiencing the frustration of the painfully slow promotion process that plagued all Victorian armies. After twenty-five years, Frederick Roberts had only attained the rank of major in the Indian Army. Most armies were filled with elderly captains who impeded the progress of all below them. Probably the most extreme example of frustrated progress was to be found in the US Army. Augustus Tassin ended the Civil War as a Brevet Brigadier General of Volunteers but, having transferred into the regular army, retired twenty years later having reached the dizzy heights as a full lieutenant.[3]

Curling continues:

This is by far the most civilised town in Africa and is extremely pretty. All the cottages (there are no houses) stand in gardens and every street has a stream of water running through it. The Governor's House is about the size of Augusta Lodge and rather resembles it in appearance.[4]

The town is in a large valley and consequently very hot, the change from Kokstadt being very great. How we shall manage this summer, I don't know, as the tents, from constant wear, have got as thin as paper. I'm afraid that so much money has been spent this year that the government at home will not sanction another little war to be paid in this year's estimates. Should this be the case, we shall be kept hanging on here until next February as it seems to be the general impression that the Zulus must be beaten before the troops leave the colony.

All the natives are made to clothe themselves before they can come into the town giving the streets quite a civilised look. There are no native women in the town at all and the men do everything. All the nurses are Niggers and it looks very funny to see a great black brute carrying a baby. The General is here now and has us out twice a week to get the spirits out of the men, I believe. Should the war not come off, he is pretty certain to return home before the year is over.

I see by this week's (London) Gazette I have got six steps but there have not been any for a very long time and to be promoted, I must have 60 steps this year, a number a long way short as yet. Now we are stationary again, the men are all going sick, a very large number have got rheumatism and several have fever. They seem to have capital health on the move but these standing camps are always unhealthy.

29th September 1878 Petermaritzburg To Mama

I have no news to tell you at all as everything is at a standstill: nothing can be done until we get some rain so that there may be grass for the bullocks. At present the country is perfectly bare, not a blade of grass to be seen anywhere.

From all the preparations that are made and the quantity of the stores collected, it is quite evident that the government intends to get the Zulu War over but there is no chance of any move being made for the next two months. This little town is crammed with troops and quite spoilt by them. We are living in the greatest discomfort, being in tents and having to be properly dressed and shaved just like all troops in garrison. Of course there is no room at the only mess in the place (*the Buffs'*), so we have to continue to piggy in our tents.

It is intensely hot, too, now as Maritzburg lies in a large valley. The thermometer in my tent goes up to 107 in the middle of the day and, as we have nowhere to go, we feel the heat very much. We are very near the equator now and have the sun nearly right overhead. Curiously, no one is sick so the heat cannot be unhealthy. I have had a touch of some fever & have lost about a stone in weight since we have been here doing nothing. It is impossible to get anything to do here in the way of exercise, there is no lawn tennis and no rides, as the country is perfectly barren, so we do nothing but ride to the Band every day.

In contrast, Colonel Wood in his camp in the north of the colony, encouraged and organized contests like tug-of-war and foot races to keep his command fit and from getting bored.

We hear no rewards of any kind are to be given until the Zulu business is over. It is rather hard as some of us have been continually at work for more than six months in Cape Colony and will be put on the same footing as men who are coming out now.

Everything is in full bloom now as it is the spring in this country. There are a few nice people but such a large garrison quite swamps the place and soldiers are looked upon as a nuisance.

Sir Bartle Frere arrived on Thursday and has a levee tomorrow, to which we shall all have to go. If I get the opportunity, I will give him my letter of introduction.

In fact, Curling and his comrades did receive some recognition in the form of the date bar on their South African War medal, which reads '1878–79'.

Henry's father continuously tried to help in influencing his son's advancement. He lobbied acquaintances with the slightest connection with the War Office or Army, but with no success. Henry was more sanguine about things for he knew he stood no chance until he was in the list of top twenty subalterns. There were no more references to this letter of introduction, which must have become somewhat dog-eared, having been carried on campaign for nine months:

> . . . Should this war come off, great losses are anticipated both from fighting and sickness. Also Zululand is near the coast and is subject to African fever and the fighting is certain to be in that part.
>
> We have shifted our camp to the top of a hill where, although it is cooler, we are nearly blown away.
>
> The Governor of this colony is a Bulwar. I suppose the same family as Lord Lytton. He is a bachelor and very unsociable, besides being an awful Cad.
>
> I heard Colenso preach last Sunday and was disappointed, as I expected something startling. We have got three bishops here. How absurd, is it not? Colenso is the best of the lot and is a nice gentlemanly old man.

Sir Henry Lytton Bulwer (1836–1914) was a career diplomat who, at the time of the Zulu War, was Lieutenant Governor of Natal. During his term, he had developed a good relationship with King Cetshwayo of the Zulus. Bulwer's views and aims, therefore, were completely at odds with those of Sir Bartle Frere's, who outranked him.

As Bulwer was opposed to a war with the Zulus, one can only interpret Curling's disdain as being coloured by this stand:

7th October 1878 Petermaritzburg To Mama

> . . . I am all right though we have been nearly suffocated by the intense heat, 97 deg in the shade.
>
> We are still in tents with no prospects of putting a roof over us as long as we remain in the country. The General has gone away to the frontier and it is quite certain that no operations can commence for at least two months, so here we shall continue to grill until there is some sickness, when we shall be moved off. Your letters continue to arrive most regularly and now that Sir Bartle Frere is here, they come weekly which is a great improvement.
>
> Our present C.O is the hardest master I ever had and keeps us

in camp every day till three and every third day, all day. He is a very indifferent officer and has no idea beyond pipeclay.

Curling and his artillery comrades were placed under the overall command of Colonel Charles Knight Pearson (1834–1909). A Crimean veteran, he rose to command the Buffs and was regarded as a steady and dependable commander rather than inspirational. He would shortly relinquish his regimental responsibilities to take command of the No.1 Coastal Column that would invade Zululand. By a matter of a few hours, they would fight and win the first battle of the war by the banks of the Nyezane River. Soon after, Pearson's Column would occupy and fortify the hilltop mission at Eshowe, where they became besieged for seventy-two days. By the time they were relieved in April there had been twenty-four fatalities, mostly from disease. Pearson's own health was broken and he was invalided home.

23rd October 1878 Petermaritzburg To Mama

We are rather gay here and have plenty of small dances, luncheon parties and amateur dramatics.

Unfortunately, the ladies out-number the gentlemen three to one so there is not much dancing to be got.

[*Henry must have meant to say that the men outnumbered the women.*]

We are in utter darkness as to whether there is to be any fighting or not. But it depends on whether Dizzy wishes to amuse the public with another little war.

Curling was wrong in thinking that the Conservative Prime Minister, Benjamin Disraeli, was even contemplating a war in South Africa. With a war with Afghanistan threatening stability in India and increasing pressure for Irish Home Rule, the British Government had plenty on its plate without looking for another confrontation. Henry, like the other male Curlings, was a Liberal and blamed the Tories for getting Britain involved in the current spate of wars.

If you want to hear anything about this place, read Lady Barker's 'House Keeping in Natal'; it will tell you far more truthfully about the country than I can and is very amusing. She lived, as I suppose you know, at this place.

I was introduced to old Colenso the other day and went to call on him yesterday. He is a very fierce old fellow, quite a peg above all the other colonial Bishops I have met. There are three of them here and two of them have what they called cathedrals with Dean, Canon, Pribends (?) etc. The biggest one of the two, which is not so large as St. Mary's at home.

Since we have been here everything has gone up 50% in price, and the town is nearly starved out as nothing can come up from the sea now. Dinner claret is 5/- a bottle, bottled beer 2/- and jam 1/6d a tin (as there is no butter, we all eat jam).

31ˢᵗ October 1878 Maritzburg To Mama

We have just got orders to march to the Zulu frontier and are to go tomorrow, so I send a few lines to say good-bye in case there may not be any regular post from the place we are going to. While we have been here there has been nothing to write about, but perhaps now there are more stirring times before us.

The extreme discomfort has quite spoiled our stay here. Now we shall be able to go in for a regular camp life again & wear beards again etc.

We got out of the house by paying a months hire and think ourselves fortunate. It was a six roomed cottage and the rent was £10 a month unfurnished, a great deal of money. Everything is at famine prices and rents are quite 100% higher than in ordinary times.

As I expect you know, the campaign against a chief called Socociene (sic) has failed utterly and fears are entertained that the Zulu King may attack us before we are ready for him, so all troops are being moved to the Frontier.

Sekhukhune (or Sekukuni) was chief of the Pedi clan whose land was in the disputed territory between northern Zululand and the Boer republic of the Transvaal. As a preliminary to the invasion of

Zululand, it was decided to neutralize Sekukuni and his troublesome tribe by sending a force under the command of Colonel Hugh Rowlands. Beset by sweltering temperatures, a dwindling water supply and a lack of forage for the draught animals, Rowlands decided to abort his advance when his column was within sight of Sekukuni's mountain stronghold. For this, Rowlands was heavily criticized and sidelined for the rest of the campaign.

The rain, or rather the want of it, keeps everything back and until it falls it is impossible to do anything against the Zulus. There is no doubt that should it come to fighting, we shall have severe work. We have no native auxiliaries in this country and the natives (Zulus) are well armed and outnumber us 100 to 1.

I will write again as soon as we halt anywhere and you will probably get the two letters at the same time as there is no steamer for the next two weeks.

We were all taken by a photo man here but they were failures & not worth sending, besides, we all took off our beards the day we came here as the Col. in command will not allow them (*Colonel Pearson of the Buffs*).

We do not know where we are going, but it is somewhere on the river Tugela and we march through a place called Greytown that I think is marked on Papa's map . . . Tell Papa there is every probability of my being promoted next January and that a Col. Hay has been made Adjutant General, with a Col. King next to him.

15th November 1878 Greytown, Natal Letter to Mama

We were kept waiting at Pietermaritzburg for transport until last Thursday and in much discomfort because everything was packed up and we were ordered to start whenever the wagons arrived. They turned up at about 4 o'clock on Thursday after-noon so we started an hour later in a heavy rain, but the roads were so slippery we only went a mile or two out of town before halting for the night. It took us five days to come this little distance on account of the incessant rain, which is very welcome all the same.

# The Curling Letters of the Zulu War

This is a pretty little village with about 20 houses but the number of troops that have been here have eaten up everything and there is not an egg or any vegetables to be had.

We provided ourselves with three months stock of provisions before starting as we shall have no opportunity of getting anything at all when we once leave here. I don't believe that the General will ever be able to advance beyond the Frontier as it is impossible to move sufficient supplies for the number of troops required.

The slow build-up to the war, which filled Curling and his fellow officers with impatience, was necessary because of the logistical complexities of moving and supplying such a large army in the field. Chelmsford and his transport officers had to buy or hire 27,000 draught oxen and 5,000 mules to haul over 2,500 wagons and employ a small army of civilian teamsters, drovers and assistants. Transport was Chelmsford's biggest headache throughout the whole campaign and constituted the greatest single expense when the cost of the war was totted up.

The long drought caused a further delay because of the lack of forage along the lines of march. The coming of the rains solved this problem but brought with it another problem. The rock-hard, dusty terrain soon became a quagmire as hundreds of men and beasts struggled through the mud. Dried out watercourses became rushing torrents which had to be crossed. This was just to get men and supplies to the border, let alone to cross it into the unknown Zulu country.

I dined with the Governor, Sir Henry Bulwer the night before we started. It was a small party, only fourteen but included the General and Sir Bartle Frere. The latter is a very urbane, benevolent looking old gentleman. He disappeared directly after dinner, on the plea of business. It was a very stiff, stupid party and we did not get up from the table until 11 o'clock. There does not seem the slightest possibility of anything taking place for another month or two and everybody, including the staff and the special officers who come out from England are very tired of the discomfort of camp life. There are now more than 5000

78

regular troops on the frontier without counting the native auxiliaries, so really we have quite an imposing force to commence operations with. Our old friends, the 90ᵗʰ Regiment, with whom I have been ever since we arrived in the colony, have left us and gone up to Utrecht, a place in the North and we are now with the 24ᵗʰ Regiment now. They seem very good fellows but, of course, we don't know them as well as the 90ᵗʰ as yet.

Sir Henry Bulwer is comparatively a young man and probably got his appointment more from his name than his talents. His secretary is a very good fellow named Seymour Hadow and is, I believe, the son of a doctor.

What bad luck it is being away from England this year with so much that interests me taking place. I am thinking this will arrive about Christmas Day. May you all have many happy returns of it. I have only missed being with you once before and I hope this may the last time. We hope to spend Christmas in Zululand but wherever we are, it will be a great day for us.

I am glad to hear by your last letter that Papa is pretty well now. I hope the wedding will not upset him. The electric light business must interest him very much. I wonder if there is anything in it. Anyway, it must make him feel very comfortable knowing the Ramsgate Gas Works are disposed of at a good price ... How uncommonly glad he must feel about the Gas business: I see the shares have fallen 20 per cent or more in some companies.

This Afghan War will absorb all the attention of the papers. There is not a single correspondent out here, although the amount of money the Government is spending must be enormous.

1879 was to become 'The Year of Electricity'. Sir Joseph Swan and Thomas Edison successfully demonstrated their versions of the filament light bulb and by the end of the year, the first electric street lighting was in operation along the Embankment and Waterloo Bridge. Although Britain was slow to develop its electrical industry, the future of gas for lighting was in decline. In this respect, Curling's father had shown good business sense in selling his business before electricity had become established.[5]

The invasion of Zululand was considered of so little significance

that only one of the London newspapers bothered to send a correspondent to cover it. Ex-officer, Charles Norris-Newman, of the
*London Standard* also acted as a 'stringer', or casual reporter, for
the local newspaper, the *Times of Natal* as well as the *Cape Standard
and Mail*. As soon as his report of the Isandlwana disaster appeared
in the *London Standard*, public interest swung away from events on
the North-West Frontier. Correspondents were hastily reassigned to
Natal and, for the next few months, reports from Zululand dominated the newspapers.

21$^{st}$ November 1878 Greytown To Mama

We are longing for the war to begin: it seems as if it never would
and should it not come off, we may be kept here for another year
on the frontier without any chance of coming home. There seems
to be no promotion going: last year, I got 75 steps, this year only
35 up to the end of September a great falling off.

Col. Turner, who commanded at Aldershot when I was there,
married the daughter of the late Lord St. Leonards and was much
pleased at the will being upset, as it brought a good deal of money
to his wife. I suppose all the money, instead of going to the eldest
son, is divided among the family so they must be all well off.

The rains have fairly set in now and there is a thunderstorm
regularly every afternoon. I enjoy it much better than the intense
heat we had before . . . Our only amusement here is snipe
shooting: we go out nearly everyday and the marshes are in
consequence getting quite depopulated. There are a few buck
and when we get into Zululand we hope to get plenty. People at
home seem to confound the Zulu country with Kaffir Land: they
are 600 miles apart and as different in every way as England and
Spain.

11$^{th}$ December 1878 Greytown To Mama

There is only a fortnightly mail regularly and no extra mail
has been advertised, so I am afraid you will have been three
weeks with out hearing from me when you get this. Lately your
letters have been arriving regularly every week as the carriers

have been constantly coming up from the coast with troops and stores, but unfortunately they don't return with any regularity. Nothing has been going on here to write about but preparations have steadily been made and the campaign will open in another three weeks. No one at home seems to have any idea what a lot of money is being spent and how extensive the preparations have been. Altogether there must be quite 10,000 troops on the frontier, including the Naval Brigade and the native regiments.

At the beginning of the War, the Naval Brigade was made up of 174 men and officers, plus forty-three Marines, of the 3,000-ton corvette HMS *Active*. The crew from another corvette, HMS *Tenedos*, shortly joined her. This force was part of Colonel Pearson's No.1 Column.

> The natives are being armed and formed like European Regiments and have the same proportion of officers. I see a soldier named Birkett has got a commission in one of them; perhaps he is the son of the Birkett we formally knew.[6] A very large number of officers have come out from England and seize all the appointments, cutting all Regimental officers out of everything. They are called Bumvogels (vultures) and get every appointment there is to be had.

The native regiments were the hastily and minimally trained Natal Native Contingent, which were recruited from among disaffected Zulus who opposed Cetshwayo. They were armed with spears and clubs, although some did have old firearms, which, in their inexpert hands, made them more lethal to their own side than to the enemy. To identify them as allies, they wore a red strip of cloth around their head or tied to their upper arms.

Some of the special service officers were given commissions to these units but they were not particularly sought after appointments. The officers held their native soldiers in contempt and no attempt was made to train them into effective fighting units.

Some commanders like Colonel Anthony Durnford, Royal Engineers, had plans to make 1st Regiment NNC into a worthwhile command, but brutish battalion commanders like Commandant

Hamilton-Browne scuppered any chance of success. One special-service officer who did make an effort was Lieutenant Henry Harford, 99th Regiment, who spoke fluent Zulu and tried to encourage and communicate with his men.

It did not help matters that the NCOs appointed were low calibre whites, who could not speak Zulu and were entirely unfitted for the task.

The *Bumvogels*, referred to by Curling, were officers who applied for leave from their regiments and travelled to Natal to volunteer for any vacancy open. Because of the chronic shortage of Transport Officers, many, like Lieutenant Horace Smith-Dorrien of the 95th Regiment, were accepted, despite having no experience. Local contractors had a field day over-charging and running rings around these inexperienced Imperial officers as they wrestled with complexities of the transport system.

> I send you a pamphlet describing the Zulu army that we are to attack. Everybody seems to think they will make a stubborn fight at first so we shall have probably severe losses on our side. They are ten times as numerous as the tribes we fought against in the last war and have never yet been defeated. No one has the least doubt that the fight will come off. Our ultimatum has been sent to the Zulu King, but it asks so much that he cannot, even if he wishes, give in. The only thing the natives understand is force. They will promise anything but always break their promises, so the only thing to be done is to take all their cattle, burn all their huts and kill a few thousand of them; if they make a fight and get beaten, so much the better. This is the way they treat one another and is the only way to keep them quiet.

On 11 December beneath two large fig trees standing on the Natal bank of the Tugela River, a charade was played out. A large party of Zulu emissaries were received by a party of dignitaries and subjected to the three-hour reading of an ultimatum prepared by Sir Bartle Frere. In it were thirteen demands to be met within twenty to thirty days, most of which were calculated to be rejected. Among the impossible demands were that the Zulu army be disbanded and the military system abandoned.

As intended, the ultimatum was rejected and the way was now open for war.

> We are in camp with the 2nd Battalion of the 24th Regiment and our column, when we march into Zululand, will consist of two Battalions of the 24th, a couple of native regiments, about 500 Cavalry & our 6 guns. I have no chance of getting an independent command. All the columns are large and have at least six guns with each, so I cannot possibly be alone, more particularly that there are so many officers senior to me out here.
>
> There are seven regiments on the frontier now, the two Battalions of the 24th, the Buffs, the 90th L.I, the 13th L.L, the 80th and the 88th. Besides this, there is the Naval Brigade and mounted corps of volunteers and irregulars and the native contingent. I'm afraid all this must be rather stupid to you but, of course, we think of nothing else as there is no chance of home until everything is over.

During the next four weeks, men and supplies were moved forward to their jumping-off points along the border. Reducing the number of columns from five, Chelmsford planned a three-pronged invasion with the central column advancing directly to the Zulu capital, Ulundi, while the left and right columns of Wood and Pearson respectively would converge from the north and south. Chelmsford's ponderous columns were separated by dozens of miles and could be attacked individually without compromising the main object of defending the king and his capital. This did not seem to be a threat at the time for it was felt that both Wood and Pearson would draw off sufficient warriors for Chelmsford to comfortably deal with Cetshwayo's over-stretched army.

Curling and his colleagues began to join the great assembly of the central column, first at Helpmakaar, their advanced depot on a bleak escarpment above the border. They then descended the twelve miles to the sprawling camp by their crossing point at Rorke's Drift.

# The Curling Letters of the Zulu War

Notes

1 *Campaigns of a War Correspondent* by Melton Prior, p. 88.
2 *Washing of the Spears* by Donald Morris, 1ˢᵗ Edition, Simon & Schuster, 1965, p. 192.
3 *Foreign Officers on the Frontier* by Brian Best. The English Westerner's Society, 1988.
4 Augusta Lodge was the Curling's home in Augusta Road. When Curling's parents died during the 1880s, Willy changed the name to Chylton Lodge.
5 *AZWHS*, June 2000, p. 91.
6 Captain R. C. Birkett served in the 2ⁿᵈ Natal Native Contingent, who were all but annihilated at Isandlwana.

# Chapter Six

# Isandlwana

Rorke's Drift was a fordable crossing point on the Buffalo River when the river normally meandered quietly over its rock-strewn bed, but the recent heavy rains had transformed it into a swollen, swift-moving flow. Now the invading army would have to be carried across by two fixed, flat-bottomed ferry platforms called ponts, which had been built and operated by the men under the supervision of Lieutenant Francis McDowell of the Royal Engineers. About a quarter of a mile away on the slope beneath a prominent hill called the Oskarsberg, known as Shiyane to the Zulus, was the Swedish mission that had been requisitioned by the Army. This was to be the forward supply depot and hospital for the central column.

B Company of 2/24th Regiment under the command of Lieutenant Gonville Bromhead was detailed to remain behind to guard the post. This was not a duty generally welcomed by the men of B Company who felt they had been penalized because their commanding officer was deaf and not well regarded by his superiors.

The 130 men of N Battery, now commanded by the newly elevated Lieutenant Colonel Harness, arrived and went into camp below the mission station. Apart from Harness and Smith, Curling's fellow officers were Lieutenants W.J. Fowler, and C.S.B. Parsons. The Battery was stationed alongside the 3rd NNC and remained there for a week, gazing across the Buffalo River at the brooding hills of

Zululand. In between the torrents of rain and low cloud, it would have been possible to make out, on the horizon, a distinctively shaped mountain, which the Zulus called *Isandlwana*.

After months of preparation and rumour, the invasion finally got under way when bugles aroused the camp at two in the morning of 11 January. In thick mist and drizzle, the soldiers and wagons began assembling by the river. Curling and the rest of N Battery were positioned on a knoll overlooking the proceedings and from where they could give covering fire if needed.

Chelmsford's central column was a formidable force made up of seven companies of 1/24th, eight companies of 2/24th, two squadrons of mounted infantry, 200 Natal Mounted Volunteers, 120 Natal Mounted Police, No.1 Company Native Pioneers, 2/3rd Natal Native Contingent, half a company of Royal Engineers, two rocket tubes from 11 Battery/7th Brigade and six 7-pounder guns of Curling's Battery. In addition there were over 300 wagons and carts driven by their teamsters, conductors and *voorlopers*, as well as clerks, servants and various camp followers.

All day, the ponts ferried men and wagons to the Zulu bank completely unopposed. Curling wrote:

Jan.18th 1879. Col. Glyn's Column, Rorke's Drift To Mama

I suppose you will see by the papers long before you get this that we have crossed into Zululand and have begun a war with the Zulus.

We left Greytown a week ago and have been moving constantly ever since and as it has been raining almost perpetually all the time we had a pretty miserable time of it. The day before yesterday all the columns crossed into Zululand. Ours, which is about 4,000 strong had to cross a river running like a millrace and about 100 yards wide. There was only one boat so although we were on the banks at 3 in the morning and the boat worked all night we did not cross until yesterday afternoon. (*Curling means 12 January, the day after the rest of the column crossed*). Fortunately the Zulus had all retreated and gave us no trouble. They left behind them nearly 300 head of cattle which we captured which means £5 each at least.

# Isandlwana

A small party of 50 or 60 took refuge among some rocks and managed to knock over 20 of our men before they were killed, so they got some fight in them.

The day after the crossing of the Buffalo, Chelmsford ordered the storming of a stronghold in the cliffs above a gorge through which the column travelled. This homestead belonged to Chief Sihayo, who was absent at the time. A sharp action, in which Sihayo's men scattered, left thirty Zulu dead for the loss of two NNC killed and three whites wounded. Curling's casualty list was somewhat exaggerated:

The total number of troops that have gone into Zululand amounts to 13,000 a sufficient number to beat them 10 times over. The General wishes to advance cautiously leaving a Depot behind here so the numbers in front will soon be reduced. We are pretty certain to have a few engagements before the Zulu's give in and take to the bush. They are well armed and have never yet fought against white men. We have got much of all our baggage and my bit consists now of a change of clothing and two blankets on a waterproof sheet. I only hope the campaign may not last long and that we may be on our way back in two or three months. Many thanks for Papa's kind message about the money. I am extremely well off out here for the simple reason that there is nothing to spend money on. We have cut down the Mess stores to whiskey and bacon and we have only got a months supply of that.

I hope you have not suffered from the journey to the South (*France*). I have expecting every day to hear about your arrival there. There is no regular post and it is quite a chance whether you get a letter or not. We don't know what the other columns have been doing as no communication lines have been opened with them as yet. We are unfortunate in our Brigadier (*Col. Richard Glyn*) but having a General with us makes it a little better. Col. Wood is by far the best man and his column will be certain to see most fighting. I cannot tell you how glad we are to swap camp life for a campaign.

One never feels fatigue when hard at work with some

excitement to keep you up. The Hospital arrangements are A1, nearly all the medicos are civilians who have been in England for six months.

They are so keen and are in every way very superior to the ordinary Army doctor. I hope Papa is better for the change and doesn't find it very dull.

Following the deceptively easy victory over Sihayo's clan, the central column continued its slow progress towards Ulundi, held back by the need to build and repair the road. It took a full nine days to reach the base of Isandlwana, just a dozen miles from Rorke's Drift. It must have been a relief to leave behind the valleys and gorges through which they had struggled and reach what seemed the perfect spot to camp. The 100 feet high rocky outcrop stood sheer above a wide valley giving an excellent view of the surrounding countryside, with undulating hills in the distance.

Chelmsford chose to erect his tents on the eastern front slope of the mountain, set out in precise rows with avenues separating the different regiments. The wagons were parked next to 'tent town', on the nek, which ran toward a small hillock called Black's or Stony Koppie. Choosing to ignore the advice from experienced colonials, Chelmsford did not form his wagons into a protective laager on the grounds that he intended to move on soon and the trouble of manoeuvring such unwieldy vehicles was not worth the faint risk of attack. The wagons would also be in constant use in bringing up supplies from Rorke's Drift. He also may have felt that his position with its panoramic view of the surrounding country was defence enough against a surprise attack.

On 21 January, Chelmsford sent out a mounted patrol under the command of an experienced ex-Imperial officer named Major John Dartnell. He was to investigate an area eight miles to the south-east and to report back. Instead, Dartnell, who had seen groups of Zulus in the hills, ignored these instructions and bivouacked for the night. He sent a messenger back to Chelmsford saying he had seen Zulus and requested reinforcements.

Chelmsford came to the conclusion that Dartnell had come upon the main Zulu army and decided to march out with half his command unencumbered by wagons. He left Lieutenant Colonel Henry Pulleine of 1/24th in charge, with instructions to be ready to strike camp next day and to follow on.

Chelmsford and Glyn left in the early hours of 22 January taking with them four guns of N Battery.

All the RA officers, including Harness and Smith accompanied Chelmsford, with the exception of Henry Curling, who was left as the officer in charge of the other two guns, equipment and seventy artillerymen in camp.

In an undated letter, probably written in mid-February, Curling describes the hours before the battle:

I was left in camp alone with my two guns, an order being given at 2 in the morning for all the force, except for the 1/24th Regt. and two guns, to start at daylight. I got up about 6 and looked after the horses left in the camp. At 7.30, I got a message to turn out at once and we got ready in about 10 minutes, forming up by the 1/24th on their parade ground. The companies were very weak, no more than 50 in each, and there were only 6 of them in all. We congratulated ourselves on the chance of our being attacked and hoped that our small numbers might induce the Zulus to come on. They were then 1,000 or 2,000 strong on some hills about 2 miles off. I suppose that not more than half the men left in camp took part in its defence as it was not considered necessary and they were left in as cooks etc. We remained outside the 24th camp for 3 hours and all had breakfast together. There must have been twenty of us altogether and not one escaped (*the officers of the 1/24th*).

The 1/24th had been in the last war and had often seen large bodies of Caffirs before. Not one of us dreamt that there was the least danger and all we hoped for was the fight might come off before the General returned. In the meantime, our dinner had been cooked and as there seemed no chance of our being attacked, we broke off and went into our tents.

When we turned out again about 12, the Zulus were only showing on the left of our camp. All the time we were idle in the camp, the Zulus were surrounding us with a huge circle several miles in circumference and hidden by hills from our sight. We none of us felt the least anxious as to the result for, although they came on in immense numbers, we felt it was impossible they could force a way through us.

This last paragraph confirms the total lack of concern on the part of the British in dealing with a frontal attack. So much so, that half of the fighting men available were either stood down or performing camp duties prior to dismantling the tents in order to break camp and go and join the rest of the column.

A patrol of the Natal Native Horse was pursuing small groups of Zulus in the hills about four or five miles to the east of the camp, when they breasted a ridge and saw a sight that made their blood run cold. A force of 20,000 warriors, who had camped undetected within five miles of the British position, were now advancing towards the camp, and the scouts were in their way. It had not been the Zulu's intention to mount an attack that day for the night of the 22–23 January was the new moon and a 'dead moon' was a bad omen. The army had intended to rest until the following day before attacking. Having learned that the British had divided their force and left the main camp totally unprepared, they quickly organized themselves into the classic Zulu formation of the buffalo chest and horns and began to advance on the ill-prepared camp.

The British would have seen the hills only two miles to their front turn black like lava pouring down the slopes. These were the impis of the chest and left horn. The Zulus, unbeknown to the British, had thrown out their right horn in a wide arc hidden by the high ground so that they approached behind Isandlwana and into the unguarded rear of the camp.

With the only organized defence spread out some 1,000 yards away with their backs to the camp and unable to fall back to a defensive position, the battle could only have one conclusion – complete annihilation.

What followed from Curling was an undated (probably 23 January) and hastily scrawled note:

My Dear Mama

Just a line to say I am alive after a most wonderful escape.
In the absence of the General, our camp was attacked by over-

whelming numbers of Zulus. The Camp was taken and out of a force of 700 white men only 30 escaped. All my men except me were killed and the guns taken. Major Smith who was with me was killed. The whole Column has retreated into Natal again and we are expecting hourly to be attacked.

Of course everything has been lost, not a blanket left.

The events that led to Henry Curling's brief note have become known as the greatest British military disaster of Queen Victoria's reign. The effect it had on its survivors, the rest of the army and the British public was traumatic, which time was slow to heal. It was all the more shocking for it was so unexpected. It seemed inconceivable that modern firepower had been swept aside by a primitively armed, half-naked and unsophisticated enemy. A defeat at the hands of a European foe would have been more readily accepted.

Henry wrote another letter to his mother dated 2 February, which went into greater detail about the beginning of the battle. Curling's hasty note was taken by an officer carrying the official dispatch to Pietermaritzburg, but it probably did not arrive at his home in Ramsgate until early March. The official dispatch, on the other hand, was telegraphed to Cape Town and carried by special steamer to St Vincent, Cape Verde Islands, whence it was telegraphed to London. This meant that news of the Isandlwana was in the newspapers by 11 February at least three weeks before the Curling family received Henry's note that he was safe. One can imagine the anxiety experienced by all at Chylton Lodge. In fact, only brother Willy was in Ramsgate and he telegrammed his parents who had decamped to the South of France for the winter:

Now things have quietened down again a little, I can tell you more about what happened. I trust you have had no false report: I saw the first man who went into Pietermaritzburg with the news and I hope you may have had no anxiety.

On the morning of the fight, the main body left at 3.30 in the morning, a little before daylight, leaving us with 2 guns and about 70 men. About 7.30, we were turned out as about 1000 Zulus were seen in some hills about 2 miles from the camp. We did not think anything of it and I was congratulating myself on having an independent command. I had out with my guns only 20 men, the remainder, 50 in number, stayed in the camp. We remained formed up in front of the camp (it was about ½ mile long) until 11 o'clock, when the enemy disappeared behind some hills to out left, we returned to camp. We none of us had the least idea that the Zulus contemplated attacking the camp and, having in the last war often seen equally large bodies of the enemy, never dreamed they would come on. Besides, we had about 600 troops (regulars), two guns, about 100 other white men and at least 1,000 armed natives.

At about 12, as the men were getting their dinner, the alarm was again given and we turned out at once. Maj. Smith came back from the General's force at this time and took command.

Brevet Major Stuart Smith had returned with Captain Alan Gardner of the staff, who had brought Lord Chelmsford's message for Colonel Pulleine to decamp and move to join the rest of the column. Curling had taken the two guns about 400 yards to the left front when Smith joined him and took over command:

This of course relieved me of all responsibility for the movement of the guns. We, being mounted, moved off before the infantry and took up a position to the left front of the camp where we were able to throw shells into a huge mass of the enemy that remained almost stationary.

From a small rise, the guns opened fire at about 1,000 yards, the limit of the 7-pounders' range and it is unlikely that they caused many casualties.[1] Curling went on to explain, 'The 24th Regt. came up and formed in skirmishing order on both our flanks,' (*Lieutenant Porteous' A Company were to the left and H Company under Lieutenant Wardell on the right.*)

The Zulus soon split up into a large mass of skirmishers that extended as far around the camp as we could see. We could get no idea of numbers but the hills were black with them. They advanced steadily in the face of the infantry and our guns, but I believe the whole of the natives who defended the rear of the camp soon bolted and left only our side of the camp defended.

As the Zulus moved nearer, Smith took one of the guns to a position a little to the right where a threat was developing. He fired a few rounds, including one that demolished a hut, before returning to his original position. It was estimated that the two guns fired off about twenty-five rounds, some of which caused many casualties. Some of the Zulus took notice of the loading drill and that, when the gun was ready to fire, the crew stood aside. At this point, the warriors threw themselves to the ground as the shot passed overhead. By now the Zulus were closing in fast on Curling's position.[2]

Very soon bullets began to whistle about our heads and the men began to fall. The Zulus still continued to advance and we began to fire case, but the order was given to retire after firing a round or two.

At this time, out of my small detachment, one man had been killed, shot through the head, another wounded, shot through the side and another through the wrist. Maj. Smith was also shot through the arm but was able to do his duty. Of course, no wounded man was attended to, there was no time or men to spare. When we got the order to retire, we limbered up at once but were hardly in time as the Zulus were on us at once and one man was killed (stabbed) as he was mounting the seat on the gun-carriage. Most of the gunners were on foot as there was no time to mount them on the guns.

Someone gave the order for the 24th Regiment to fall back and take up a defensive position closer to the camp. This momentarily left the artillery exposed as they hurried to limber up the guns and fall back with the infantry. It must have been a terrifying moment as the unarmed gunners without horses attempted to mount the limbers that could carry them away from the hordes of warriors who quickly overran their position. As the drivers whipped the draughthorses,

Smith and Curling, both mounted on artillery chargers, led the frantic retreat, which left those crew without horses to run for the camp and hope, in vain, that they could outpace their fearsome pursuers. None survived. The two guns bounced and crashed their way across the uneven ground to the camp and reached the tents of the 2/24th.

Captain Essex mentioned in his evidence to the Court of Enquiry:

'. . . It was now about 1.30 p.m., about this period, 2 guns with which Major Smith and Lt. Curling R.A. were returning with great difficulty, owing to the nature of the ground, and I understood were just a few seconds late.'

Expecting comparative safety, Curling was dismayed by the sight awaiting them.

'We trotted off to the camp thinking to take up another position but found it in possession of the enemy, who were killing the men as they ran out of their tents.'

J.F. Brickhill, employed as an interpreter, left one of the most graphic descriptions of the moment the Zulus overwhelmed the camp and the flight of the survivors:

I went round the Volunteer Camps into that of the 2/24th. Men were running everywhere but I could see no officer. I saw one of the field pieces brought to the corner of this camp. The men jumped off and took to their heels. Simultaneously with this, the only body of soldiers yet visible, rose from firing their last shot and joined in the general flight. Panic was everywhere and no officer to guide, no shelter to fall back upon . . .

The Zulus, for the last 300 yards, did not fire 25 shots, but came on with the steady determination of walking down the camp by force of numbers. I consider that they were 30 to 1 of us. At 150 yards distance, they raised a shout of 'Usutu' . . . They now came on with an overwhelming rush. I went to the head of the 1/24th camp to see if I could see anything of my companion, but could not, so seeing that the Zulus were already stabbing in this camp as well as the others, I joined the fugitives retreating over the nek, on reaching which I found all communication by the road we had come along (*from Rorke's Drift*) cut off by several lines of Zulus running across.

*Isandlwana*

Curling's account continued:

> We went right through them (*the tents*) and out the other side, losing nearly all our gunners in doing so and one of the two sergeants. .
> . . . A soldier is individually no use in this warfare. When on sentry, he cannot see a Kaffir 10 yards off and he can do nothing until he is ordered to do it. They behaved splendidly, however, in this fight. They were all killed in the ranks as they stood. Not a single man escaped from those companies that were placed to defend the camp. Indeed, they were completely cut off from any retreat and could not do so, as we did, gallop through the Zulus. When I last saw them, they were retreating steadily but I believe a rush was made and they were all killed in a few minutes.
> Both my servant and groom were in camp and escaped in a wonderful way. They both got horses and got away in their shirt sleeve (sic) and on bareback horses. (*They were Driver Elias Tucker and Gunner Green.*)

In his evidence to the Court of Enquiry a few days later, he mentions something omitted in all his letters:

> When we got to the road to Rorke's Drift, it was completely blocked by Zulus. I was with Major Smith at this time, he told me he had been wounded in the arm. We saw Lt. Coghill, the ADC, and asked him if we could not rally some men and make a stand, he said he did not think it could be done.

Lieutenant Neville Coghill of 2/24th would have been with Lord Chelmsford but for a wounded knee that had excused him from duty and kept him in camp. The wound had been caused by some horseplay in the mess some weeks before and had been aggravated when Coghill had tried to capture a chicken for the General's pot.
    Curling's letter of 2 February continues:

> The road to Rorke's Drift that we hoped to retreat by was full of the enemy so, no way being open, we followed a crowd of natives and camp followers who were running down a ravine.

95

The Zulus were all among them, stabbing men as they ran.

The ravine got steeper and steeper and finally the guns stuck and could get no further. In a moment, the Zulus closed in and the drivers, who alone remained, were pulled off their horses and killed. I did not see Maj. Smith at this moment but was with him a minute before.

(*Court of Enquiry*) . . . The Zulus were in the middle of the crowd, stabbing the men as they ran. When we had gone about 400 yards, we came to a deep cut, in which the guns stuck. There was, as far as I could see, only one gunner with them at this time, but they were covered with men of different corps clinging to them. The Zulus were in them at once and the drivers pulled off their horses. I then left the guns.

(*2 Feb*) . . . The guns could not be spiked, there was no time to think of anything and we hoped to save the guns up to the last moment.

Harness also wrote, '. . . He (*Curling*) did not leave the guns until the Zulus were upon them and then no one could have got the spikes and hammer (*the former were carried in an axel-tree box*) and used them – and it is most improbable that Smith carried the spikes in his pocket.'[3]

Lieutenant Smith-Dorrien, 95th Regiment, later wrote:

'. . . I came upon the two guns which must have been sent out of the camp before the Zulus charged home. They appeared to me to be upset in a donga and to be surrounded by Zulus . . . I caught up with Curling and spoke to him, pointing out that the Zulus were all around and urging him to push on, which he did.'

Could this seemingly obvious piece of advice mean that Curling's poor eyesight prevented him seeing just how precarious was his position? All Curling had to say was, 'As soon as the guns were taken, I galloped off and made off with the crowd. (*Court of Enquiry*) . . . Shortly after this, I saw Lt. Coghill, who told me Col. Pulleine had been killed.'

Having escaped the horrors of the camp, the survivors were about to endure the terrifying experience of running the gauntlet of several thousand fleet-footed warriors. Those unfortunates without horses were soon overtaken and killed. Even a mounted man was not safe, for the rugged terrain prevented the horses from moving much faster than a walk. The Zulus were able to run as fast and many of the horsemen were killed as they were overtaken. There has been a suggestion that those soldiers dressed in red tunics were the favourite targets for the Zulus. If so, it may explain how Curling, dressed in dark blue, managed to evade being attacked.

Again, J.F. Brickhill wrote a vivid account of the flight down what became known as the Fugitives' Trail:

> . . .Our flight I never shall forget. No path, no track, boulders everywhere – on we went, borne now into some dry torrent bed, now weaving our way amongst trees of stunted growth, so that unless you made the best use of your eyes, you were in constant danger of colliding against some tree or finding yourself un-horsed at the bottom of some ravine. Our way was already strewn with shields, assegais, blankets, hats, clothing of all description, guns, ammunition belts, saddles (which horses had managed to kick off), revolver and belt and I don't know what not. Whilst our stampede was composed of mules, with and without pack saddles, oxen, horses in all stages of equip-ment and fleeing men all strangely intermingled – man and beast, apparently all infected with the danger which surrounded us. One riderless horse that run up alongside of me I caught and gave to a poor soldier, who was struggling along on foot, but he had scarcely mounted before he was knocked off by a Zulu bullet.
>
> . . . Whilst going down into a deep dry torrent bed, I saw Lieutenants Melvill and Coghill and Conductor Foley about 200 yards ahead only more to our right. A stream of Zulus running on their right was fast pressing them down towards the course we were on. Scrambling over the rocky bed as best we could, we came up the hill on this side, fully exposed to the enemy's rear and cross fire. We here came to an abrupt halt by reason of a huge chasm or gully, which opened to view in front of our horses. There was nothing for it but to turn sharply round and follow the course of this gully down in the hopes of finding a crossing somewhere . . . We found a crossing to the gully, but so steep that on coming out on this side, I laced my arms around my horse's neck and threw my head as far forward as possible

and, even then, it will ever remain a puzzle how our horses got out of this without falling over backwards.

A little further, I found Mr. Melvill carrying the colours was just in front of me.

Curling (*Court of Enquiry*) '. . . Near the river I saw Lt. Melvill, 1/24<sup>th</sup>, with a colour, the staff being broken.'

Lieutenant Teignmouth Melvill, 1/24<sup>th</sup>, is said to have been entrusted with bringing the Queen's Colour to safety. It is thought that he left the camp just before it was finally overwhelmed, which would put his position a little behind that of Curling and Coghill.

Curling, again: 'How any of us escaped, I don't know; the Zulus were all around us and I saw men falling all around. We rode for 5 miles, hotly pursued by the Zulus, when we came to a cliff over-hanging the river.'

Those fugitives that had survived the five to six mile ride were now all bunched up in a bottleneck as they reached the Buffalo River. On the far bank they could see Natal and safety. In between there was yet another fearsome obstacle to overcome.

The survivors were forced into single file as they reached cliff tops overlooking the rain-swollen river. The Zulus had not let up in their pursuit and any delay by those in the front of the file, meant death for those at the back. Lieutenant Smith-Dorrien recalled that he was binding up the wounds of a mounted infantryman, when there was a shout behind him:

Get on with it, man, the Zulus are on top of you! . . . I turned round and saw Major Smith R.A., who was commanding the section of guns, as white as a sheet and bleeding profusely; and in a second, we were surrounded, and assegais accounted for poor Smith, my wounded MI friend and my horse. With the help of my revolver, and a wild jump down the rocks, I found myself in the Buffalo River.

Curling witnessed this incident and wrote on 2 February:

I saw several wounded men during the retreat, all crying out for help, as they knew a terrible fate was in store for them. Smith-

Dorrien, a young fellow in the 95th Regt., I saw dismount and try to help one. His horse was killed in a minute by a shot and he had to run for his life, only escaping by a miracle.

. . . We had to climb down the face of the cliff and not more than half those who started from the top, got to the bottom. Many fell right down, among others, Maj. Smith and the Zulus caught us here and shot us as we climbed down. I got down safely and came to the river, which was very swift and deep. Numbers were swept away as they tried to cross and others were shot from above.

My horse, fortunately, swam straight across, though I had three or four men hanging on his tail, stirrup leathers, etc. After crossing the river, we were in comparative safety, though many were killed afterwards who were on foot and unable to keep up. It seems like a dream, I cannot realise it at all. The whole affair did not last an hour from beginning to end. Many got away from the camp but were killed in the retreat.

None of the officers of the 24th Regt. could escape: they were all on foot and on the other side of the camp. I saw two of them, who were not with their men, near the river but their bodies were found afterwards on our side of the river.

These were the bodies of Melvill and Coghill, who were later posthumously awarded the Victoria Cross. Coghill had managed to reach the safety of the Natal bank on horseback, when he saw that Melvill was unhorsed and clinging to a large rock in mid-stream. As Coghill turned his horse to go to his comrade's help, a Zulu bullet killed his horse and threw him into the river. He managed to swim to Melvill, who had been unable to hold onto the cumbersome cased colour. Together they struggled to reach the bank and climb the steep hill until exhaustion and Coghill's lameness forced them to stop with their backs against a large rock. Here the two officers made a feeble last stand before being quickly overwhelmed and killed by natives friendly to the Zulus and who accounted for most of the fatalities on the Natal bank.[4]

Curling wrote a letter, probably in mid-February, the first page of which is missing. He largely repeats the way the battle unfolded until retreat was the only option:

# The Curling Letters of the Zulu War

. . . We tried to get away down a ravine but the moment the guns stuck the Zulus closed on them and all was over in a minute. The flight to the river is almost too terrible to describe, men running on until exhausted and then falling down & being stabbed by the Zulus. The passage of the river was even worse: not half those who tried to get across, succeeded. Many had their horses shot in the stream and so many clung to every horse that they were pulled down and unable to swim.

Poor Smith lost his life through his extreme energy: he volunteered to come back to camp to bring up provisions and arrived just in time to take part in the action. He, like many others, was wounded early in the fight and, as not a single wounded man escaped, shared their fate. He fell down some rocks near the river, probably from weakness and was too much hurt to continue the flight.

I suppose you have heard all about the recovery of one of the colours belonging to 1/24th. Melvill who was carrying it was away a long time before me but his horse, like many others, came to grief and although he crossed the river before I did, he was killed the other side. My horse never made a mistake from the beginning and swam the river without the least trouble. If he had stumbled once, it would have been all over. I was wonderfully lucky in not having my horse stabbed and can only account for it by so many men on foot affording an easier mark for the Zulus. Very few mounted men were stabbed as the Zulus cannot get at them easily. All the Zulus were quite naked and they, as is their custom, disembowelled all the wounded and dead. No one knows what was done to the numerous wounded in camp but there is every reason to believe that many were burnt. The General halted for the night in the Camp and his men slept among the dead bodies of their comrades. They were fearfully ill-treated, their faces cut to pieces and their bodies terribly cut about. I lost everything I most value in the camp. The old despatch box with letters, photos, accounts and all my little stock of studs, links etc. One ought not to think of anything after having had such a wonderful escape. As to clothing, blankets etc., there have been sales of all the kits belonging to the officers who were killed and I have been able to get the most necessary things one requires. This paper I am writing on belonged to one of the poor fellows in the 24th.

The whole of this part of South Africa is in a most disturbed state and no one knows what complications may not arise. It may take a year before these disturbances are all put down . . .

Those who survived to reach the Natal bank and evade being ambushed by the hostile Zulu allies, made their way to either Rorke's Drift or Helpmakaar. There was little or no organized attempt by the survivors to gather together and help those fugitives who reached the top of the steep slope. Demoralized and shocked, the fugitives made their way to safety individually or in small groups. To their credit, the only unit to give any covering fire were the men of the Natal Native Horse.

Curling joined a group including Cochrane, Gardner and Essex on the road to Helpmakaar, reasoning, correctly, that Rorke's Drift would most likely be attacked. Horace Smith-Dorrien was the last to arrive. Utterly exhausted, he had walked the twenty miles from the river and arrived at Helpmakaar around midnight.

Notes

1   One of history's great 'ifs' is what would have happened if the camp had been moved that day and rejoined Chelmsford's command. The Zulus had tricked the British into splitting their force but did not know they were about to decamp. If the main impi had remained undetected and attacked the following day as they had intended, they would have been confronted with a reunited force, which would have been more than capable of withstanding such an onslaught.
2   *Blood on the Painted Mountain* by Ron Lock, Hodder & Stoughton, 1983, p. 48. The Zulu army was not camped en masse in a gorge on the northern side of the Nqutu Plateau, but bivouacked, in regiments, over a distance of about four miles, all along the Nqutu hills and that the regiments attacked in the same strung-out line as that in which they were bivouacked. This would explain how the Zulu army appeared with such speed, already fanned out four miles wide, to encircle the camp.

# Chapter Seven

# Aimless Despondency

When the bedraggled and exhausted survivors reached Helpmakaar, the sight that greeted them did not comfort them. The bustling depot they had left just a fortnight before had been reduced to an unfortified wind-swept and sodden area consisting of a corrugated stores shed and a few tents belonging to a section of infantry left as guards.

As the senior officer, Captain Essex took command and organized a defence with the few tools he had at his disposal. He made a small laager by surrounding the zinc shed with the few wagons left and infilling with sacks of mealies. At this time there were forty-eight people, including volunteers, camp followers and two or three farmers with their families, who had come in for protection.

The volunteers had little enthusiasm left to fight and began to take their horses and drift away. Essex threatened to shoot the horses to stop further desertions, which lowered morale still further. Two of the men who did ride away were to become figures of controversy. Lieutenant Higginson of the NNC had been with both Melvill and Coghill as they had clung to the rock in the Buffalo River. On reaching the bank, he had promised to fetch horses for the other two. Instead, once he had found a mount, he had ridden off to safety.

Captain William Stephenson had been at Rorke's Drift with his NNC, who had worked at building the defensive barricades of sacks and boxes. As the fugitives from Isandlwana rode by, telling tales of slaughter, so the NNC deserted en masse, including Captain Stephenson. He stopped briefly at Helpmakaar before riding onto the safety of Ladysmith. He was later arrested, court martialled and dismissed.

For a few anxious hours, there were just twenty-eight rifles to defend Helpmakaar from the attack that was fully expected.

28th January 1879 Helpmakar, Zulu Border To Mama

I sent off a line directly I arrived here to let you know I had escaped from the massacre when our camp was taken. It was the most fearful thing one could imagine. There was no mail going before the one by which my letter went so I trust you will not have been anxious on my account. We have had no sleep since and had no opportunity of washing until yesterday. I am pretty well done up and another week of this will be too much. We lost everything except what we were standing in. Having saved one's life, it seems of little account. During the retreat all my men were killed and finally the guns stuck in a hole and the drivers were killed. How I escaped, I don't know. Capt. Smith got away at the same time but was killed. Out of 21 men in my detachment, 19 were killed. We left 51 men in camp, 41 of them were killed. The whole 24th Regt., officers and men were killed. We tried to save the guns and broke through the circle but could not get away. Even when the guns were taken and we tried to escape alone, only a very few succeeded as we were stabbed at for four or five miles. We had to swim a big river and numbers were drowned in doing so.

After the camp was taken, there was very little firing, the Zulus using their assegais and spears entirely.

We were pursued for 7 or 8 miles and did not know whether to go to the camp at Rorke's Drift or to come here. Fortunately, we came here as those who went to Rorke's Drift were all caught and murdered.

We did not get here until about 6 o'clock and had then to set to work at once to barricade the buildings as we expected every moment to be attacked. We were only 28 in number, so it is fortunate they did not.

## Aimless Despondency

2<sup>nd</sup> Feb.

Those who have escaped have not a rag left as they came away in their shirtsleeves. We always sleep at night in the fort or laager, as it is called, and in the open air. It is very unpleasant as it rains nearly every night and is very cold.

We none of us have more than one blanket each, so you can see we are having a rough time. The first few days I was utterly done up but have pulled round alright now.

About 12 o'clock, two companies of infantry came in, so we felt a little safer.

These were two Companies of 1/24<sup>th</sup> Regiment who returned with Major Henry Spalding, the special duty officer, from an abortive attempt to reinforce the single company at Rorke's Drift.

We heard heavy firing all night in the direction of Rorke's Drift and saw several fires. No news arrived until 12 o'clock, when we heard to our great relief that the General had got back to Rorke's Drift and occupied the farm buildings there. During the night, the Zulus attacked this farm which was only occupied by one Company of our troops but they were beaten off with a loss of 700 men or more.

Unfortunately, they succeeded in burning an outbuilding that was used as a hospital and they butchered in it 9 of our men. They also killed 5 men during the defence and wounded many others.

The defence of Rorke's Drift was a heroic feat of arms and did much to restore faith in the British soldier in the eyes of the public. A total of 139 British defenders were crowded within the makeshift barricades, including thirty-five patients in the hospital. For twelve hours this tiny command held at bay some 4,000 Zulus, sustaining only seventeen killed and eight wounded. One of the defenders was Gunner Arthur Howard, a member of N/5 and batman to Colonel Harness, who wrote of his experience:

Just a line to let you know that I am still in the land of the living. I daresay before you get this you will have heard of the massacre.

They killed just half of our battery, and nearly all the 1/24th Regiment. The awful black devils watched the General out of camp, and then, as soon as his command had got clear away, they came down like bees out of a hive, and there was awful slaughter. They took everything belonging to officers and men – all but what they stood upright in – burnt the huts and scattered the provisions all about the place. There was a great deal of money in camp – my Governor (*Col. Harness*) lost a bit, but, as it was government money to pay the battery with, he will get it back again. I was not in camp, for I had the diarrhoea and was left behind at a place they call Rorke's Drift, where there was a temporary hospital. One company of the 24th, ninety strong, was left to protect it.

Well, the same day as the other affair happened about which I have just told you, four thousand or so of them paid us a visit at the hospital. But we had about three hours notice and plenty of sacks of oats with which we threw up a temporary fortification around this old place. When the Zulus arrived, about five in the evening, they did not find it quite as comfortable as they thought, for they expected that they would have nothing to do but assegai us at their pleasure, and possess the place, but we had knocked holes through the house to fire through, we had very good cover. Boxes of ammunition were placed behind us. Forty men were in hospital, and nearly all able to fight when it came to the pinch. I had a rifle belonging to a sergeant who was too ill to use it. The Zulus made short work of him.[1]

When waiting for the approach of the enemy we would see them half a mile before they got to us. When I beheld the swarm I said to myself, 'All up now', but I was wrong, and we all agreed to fight till only two were left, and these were to shoot themselves. Well, we all got behind our rampart, and when the Zulus were about 400 yards off, like a wall coming on, we fired our first volley. The rifles, being Martini-Henrys, our firing was very quick, and, when struck by the bullets, the niggers would give a spring in the air and fall flat down. The enemy advanced to within 300 yards, and then it did not seem healthy to come any nearer, so we continued to fire at them until it got dark. Then,

106

as the roof of the hospital was of thatch, they crept up and set it on fire. When the flames burst out it was all the better for us, for we could see the niggers and their movements, though they could not see us. Didn't we give it to them then, anyhow! They sheered off, all but a few who hung about us all night; but as soon as it was light we finished off all we could see, and I can tell you that when I saw the general's column coming to our relief I was glad. The general said we were a brave little garrison, and that this showed what a few men could do if they only had pluck.[2]

Curling's letter of 2 February continues:

As soon as I heard the General was at Rorke's Drift with his column, which included the remains of the Battery, I rode there with several others and arrived just as it was getting dark.

Large masses of Zulus were appearing on the hills all around and a strong fortification had been made around the farm. We lay down round the parapets but although there were several alarms, no attack was made. None of us had any blankets and the men not even their great coats. The General and staff were no better off and as the night was cold we felt it much. The General started off at daylight for Pietermaritzburg and we left at 9 for this place where we have remained ever since.

We are little better off here as the buildings are all full of stores and everybody has to sleep in the open. The fort is only 70 yards square and 800 men sleep in it at night so you can understand how terrible the nights are.

On 29 January a company of Royal Engineers, under Captain Walter Park Jones, dug a trench and built a parapet around the sheds at Helpmakaar, which gave some semblance of a fort. A drawbridge spanned the ditch and three of the Battery's guns were placed at three corners. Jones thought the position as unsuitable as it was prone to become waterlogged whenever it rained. Indeed, after one particularly heavy downpour, the ditch was filled with water to a depth of six feet. With all the 24th now at Rorke's Drift, four companies of the 4th Regiment now defended Helpmakaar.

# The Curling Letters of the Zulu War

30th Jan.

I am much better now and quite got over those two fearful days. We are of course still living in the same way and it may be months before there will be any change as there are scarcely any tents left in the Colony. We have had only one wet night fortunately as yet but should it set in badly we should suffer very much. We have 30 sick and wounded men inside and several typhoid patients who however are left in a tent outside where of course they will at once be killed if we are attacked.

The Farm house at Rorke's Drift was a sad sight. There were dead bodies of Zulus all round it, in some places so thick that you could hardly walk without treading on them. The roof had been taken off the house as it was liable to be burnt and the wounded were lying out in the open. A spy was hanging on one of the trees in the garden and the whole place was one mass of men.

Nothing will now be done until strong reinforcements arrive and we shall have much bloodshed before it is all over. I wonder shall I ever see you again. Having had such a wonderful escape makes one hope for the best.

2nd Feb.

What is going to happen to us, no one knows. We have made a strong entrenchment and are pretty safe even should we be attacked. The only thing we are afraid of is sickness. There are 50 sick and wounded already who are jammed up at night in the fort. The smell is terrible, 800 men cooped up in so small a place. Food, fortunately, is plentiful and we have a three months supply.

All spys (sic) taken now are shot: we have disposed of three or four already. Formerly, they were allowed anywhere and our disaster is a great extent due to their accurate information of the General's movements. What excitement this will cause in England and what indignation.

In the aftermath of Isandlwana, there was a climate of suspicion and paranoia about any native caught near both Rorke's Drift and Helpmakaar. Curling had already seen a Zulu hanging from a tree at

Rorke's Drift and several natives met a similar fate at Helpmakaar, even though they were probably entirely innocent.

The suggestion that a Zulu spy network was the cause of Chelmsford's defeat was ludicrous and indicative of the wild theories and rumours circulating around the British camps. Curling was right about the shock and outrage with which the news of the disaster was received in Britain.

The campaign went from being a minor sideshow, overshadowed by the Afghan War, to one that fascinated the British public who demanded the full weight of the British army, irrespective of the cost, to exact revenge against the Zulus.

Having time to reflect, Curling wrote critically of the way the camp had been left inadequately defended:

> The troops, of course, were badly placed and the arrangements for defending the camp indifferent but there should have been enough troops and the risk of leaving a small force to be attacked by 10 to 15 times its number should not have been allowed. As you have heard, there were no wounded, all the wounded were killed in a most horrible way. I saw several wounded during the retreat, all crying out for help, as they knew the terrible fate in store for them.

Curling then went on to make a comment that later brought a storm of colonial outrage down on his head. 'You will see all sorts of accounts in the papers and no end of lies. Most of those who escaped were volunteers and native contingent officers who tell any number of lies.'

Having escaped death several times on 22 January, Curling must have felt he was entitled to some comfort and sympathy. Instead, he and the other survivors were left to fend for themselves at one of the bleakest places on the border. Lieutenant Colonel Harness accurately described this period as 'aimless despondency'. Curling's next letter echoes this despair:

7th February 1879 Helpmakar (sic), Natal To Mama

> We are still living in the greatest misery. At night, all tents are struck and we go into a small fort we have built. There is no

cover and it has been raining nearly continuously for the last three days. 800 men have made the place knee deep in mud and there is not room for all to lay down at the same time. I wonder what the end of all this will be. We all so thoroughly made up our minds that there was to be no fighting of any consequence that all plans are upset and the authorities do not seem to know what to do. We are only 6 miles in a direct line from the scene of our disaster and we can see with glasses the remains of our wagons and stores. The whole affair seems like a bad dream, too terrible to be true.

There was a Court of Enquiry held a few days ago and we all who escaped gave evidence. You will probably see all of it in print. The whole thing lasted such a short time – not more than 20 minutes from the time we retired until the guns were taken that we can hardly realise what a terrible thing it was.

We had a terrible night here on the day of the action. We fortified the stores as well as we could but men sneaked off one by one that when it was dark, we had but 37 to defend the place. In the distance we saw the light of the burning hospital at Rorke's Drift and were told that it had been taken by the enemy. Had they attacked, it would have been all up with us.

At 12 o'clock, 2 companies of Infantry came in and we felt comparatively safe. There is no doubt that the Zulus suffered a most tremendous loss. At least 4,000 or 5,000 men. They have never been opposed to Europeans before and came in masses in the face of a tremendous fire. At one time every shell I fired went into a solid mass of them and must have caused great destruction. One proof of this is that we have not been molested by them since.

The rest of N Battery was sent to Helpmakaar, where, at Chelmsford's instigation, a Court of Enquiry was convened on 27 January. The officers chosen to take the statements were Colonel F.C. Hassard, RE, Lieutenant Colonels Law and Harness, RA. The brief of the court was 'to inquire into the loss of the camp' but not to pronounce any judgement on the findings. Statements were presented by Gardner, Cochrane, Essex, Smith-Dorien and Curling, the five Imperial officers who had escaped. Evidence was also heard from

Captain Nourse of the 1/1 NNC. Both Colonel Glyn and Major Clery, who had been with Chelmsford, also made statements. The result was deliberately inconclusive, thanks to Harness's insistence. Fiercely loyal to Chelmsford, he wished to follow his chief's instructions to the letter and present stark facts without any opinions or conclusions. He later explained, 'The Court of Enquiry was assembled by Lord Chelmsford for the purpose of collecting evidence for his own information.'[3]

Harness had closely questioned Curling beforehand and made him omit all personal observations and views from his account, the result of which was a short and drily delivered report. Curling did, however, convey the sense of chaos and lack of command. In fact, in most of his dealings, Harness comes across as somewhat unsympathetic towards Curling. In a later defence of his handling of the Enquiry, Harness rather insensitively dismisses the experiences of the survivors as, '. . . doubtful particulars of small incidents more or less ghastly in their nature'. Weasel words, indeed. He does, however, acknowledge Curling's distress, '. . . his nerves were a good deal shaken'.[4]

In fairness to Harness he, too, was under stress and demoralized. Not only had he lost sixty-two men, most of his horses and two guns, all the equipment and wagons, he also grieved for the loss of his friend, Stuart Smith. This was a period when irreversible traumatic avoidance conditioning, which had been the lot of public school boys, was the expected behaviour of officers in war. In simple terms, Curling was expected to display a stiff upper lip and keep his emotions in check.[5]

Unable to offload his grief and fears to his companions or superiors, Curling resorted to the next best thing; a trio of letters to his mother, in which he repeatedly goes over the terrible events of the 22nd, as if to exorcise the terrible images trapped within himself.

There has been a suggestion that Curling suffered a breakdown, but there is no evidence of this. There were several cases where this was so, including Lord Chelmsford and Colonel Glyn, who had lost his entire regiment. Sixty-year-old Colonel Hassard RE was sent from the Cape to command Helpmakaar and to act as president of the Court of Enquiry. He found the experience too distressing and managed to be returned to Cape Town on medical grounds.[6] It should be noted that none of these officers took part in the battle but were nevertheless greatly affected by the aftermath.

## The Curling Letters of the Zulu War

The most prevalent symptom of the trauma generally displayed by the British officers was one of disinterest and inertia. Both Harness and his friend, Lieutenant Colonel John Russell, who was in command of all mounted troops, both lost interest in their commands and there were several weeks before the lethargy could be broken. Harness did recover and was able to reorganize his battery but Russell failed to send out mounted patrols and came in for much criticism. The latter was sent to Colonel Wood's command and took part in the Hlobane fiasco. Whether due to Wood's ambiguous directions or whether he just lost his nerve, Russell led his command away from the fight at a crucial moment. As a result, Russell was cast as the scapegoat for the disaster, stripped of his command and ordered to take charge of the remount depot in Pietermaritzburg.

Curling was the only Artillery officer to escape but there were eight other ranks who also managed to reach safety:

(2nd Feb) . . . Of the 50 men we left in camp, 8 managed to escape on spare horses we had left in camp. One sergeant only of my detachment, got away. Altogether, we lost 62 men and 24 horses, just half the battery.

Driver Elias Tucker wrote to his parents on 28 January which, typical of a soldier's letter, was light on details and somewhat inaccurate regarding the duration of the battle and the Zulu casualties:

. . . They came right round us, and massacred every one; and I am one of four – Sergeant Costellan (sic),
   Lieutenant Curling (that's my master) and myself and Gunner Green. We four had a horse each, and we charged right through the Zulus and cut our way out. I was in my shirtsleeves carrying ammunition to the guns.
   We lost everything in camp; they burnt everything that would burn. All our waggons and carts we had for ammunition they filled up with dead white men. They cut everyone up, and took his heart and laid it on his breast, and put his right hand in where they took his heart from, and put all the skulls in a heap. We rode a hard gallop from the time we cut our way out of camp

until four next morning, and we found ourselves in sight of Helpmakaar, and that gave us fresh strength, hoping to find some help there; but when we got there, there were only six men on guard belonging to the 13th Regiment. We frightened them out of their lives. There is only one store in Helpmakaar, and that was filled stocks of corn. We got that out and barricaded all the doors, and cut some loopholes through the sides and ends to fire through. We were afraid they would attack us here, but they have not been.[7]

There has been a considerable debate as to who the eight survivors were but probably the correct list is, Driver John Baggeley, Driver James Burchell, Sergeant John Costellow, Gunner Goff, Gunner Green, Trumpeter Nicholas Martin, Driver Edward Price and Driver Elias Tucker.[8]

For some unknown reason, Curling was not mounted on his own charger during the battle and retreat but on one of the artillery horses. He wrote on 2 October:

> . . . The horse I escaped with from Isandlwana was not my own. I never rode him until that day. Fortunately he turned out a good one and never made a mistake as so many others did. I kept him, although a very unpleasant and useless horse for my work, until he got sick and I was obliged to send him to a sick depot where he now is. He was one of the spare draught horses not used for riding purposes which makes it the more curious that he should have carried me so well that day.

Coincidentally, Major Smith also was not riding his favourite horse that day. He possibly changed mounts after riding back from Chelmsford's Column and left his horse in camp. In the confusion and panic caused when the Zulus overran the camp, Sergeant Costellow grabbed the nearest available horse, which was Smith's, and managed to ride to safety.

The clothing, kits and possessions of those killed at Isandlwana were auctioned and fetched high prices among the impoverished survivors. Amongst the lots sold was Stuart Smith's horse, which fetched £33.[9]

With so many men crammed into a small and insanitary area there was invariably an outbreak of sickness. Curling's resistance was low and he caught enteric fever, which removed him from Helpmakaar for several weeks and led to the rumour that he had suffered from a nervous breakdown. Lieutenant Colonel Harness (*Curling's C.O.*), for one, thought so. He wrote to his sister about officers who he felt were succumbing to pressure too easily. Colonel Hassard, who commanded at Helpmakaar, and his adjutant both claimed to be ill and were invalided to Cape Town, where they joined their wives. Of Curling, Harness wrote:

> You will think me still more ill-natured when I tell you that (Curling) who escaped from Isandula (sic) has gone away ill and the doctor where he has gone to says 'there is nothing the matter with him'. Poor fellow – I am afraid his nerves were a good deal shaken on 22nd January but what is to be done now? The colonel here, Colonel Glyn, has ordered him to be sent back as soon as convenient. No more ill-natured remarks at present, so goodbye.[10]

This rather carping remark reinforces the coolness and lack of sympathy Harness displayed towards Curling, for he further wrote with more understanding about other victims in his command; 'We have a great many cases of fever, not I fancy very dangerous, but a fever that seems most difficult to recover strength from . . . But the fact is it is very difficult to get well with the great discomfort a sick man must put up with, so that I send everyone I can away to Ladysmith without reference to anyone, whenever the opportunity occurs'.

Harness had been quick to recover from the trauma of Isandlwana and had reorganized the remains of his Battery until they were ready to take the field again by the beginning of April.

Curling wrote an undated letter but which was probably written in mid-February:

> . . . When I shall see you all again, if ever, I have no idea. Even if everything goes on well, not for a year at least. This fighting is not glorious work: it is dangerous as fighting against Europeans and there is little credit to be got in fighting savages. The whole of Natal is in mourning. Almost all the available young men in the colony are volunteers. They are all in the field

now and more than 100 of them were killed in this action. Many of them are Gentlemen and they set an example to regular troops in the way they stand the fatigues and drudgery of camp life.

This is quite the opposite of the disparaging comments he earlier wrote about the volunteers:

. . . Another thing that strikes me very much is how little impression the sad affair seems to make on everybody. You hear men singing just the same as if they had not lost half their number a week ago. The Officers too seem to be as cheerful and take just as much trouble about their food etc. as if nothing happened.

I trust you have had no anxiety about me: the Officer who took the official telegram down to Pietermaritzburg had a list of the Officers killed, which list we were told was telegraphed to Cape Town and sent off by special steamer to St. Vincent, where it will be wired to England.

I suppose by this time you are at Cannes, so you will not get this until long after you have seen accounts of everything in the papers . . . Willy will open this of course and then send it on to you. I hope you are all quite well and Cannes suits your health. Give my love to Papa and Emmy and believe me still able to thank God to sign myself.

There was gap of four weeks before Henry was able to resume his correspondence. When he does, the letter is written in a shakier and much larger hand than the others. The next four letters were written on a good quality notepaper bearing an unusual embossed red crest; a right arm raised with a clenched fist. As Curling mentioned in a previous letter, he had bought various items at an auction of the effects of the Isandlwana dead and the paper had belonged to an officer in the 24ᵗʰ Regiment

18ᵗʰ March 1899 Ladysmith To Mama

I am afraid I frightened you terribly when I wrote to you I had got fever. I foolishly wrote just when I was bad with fever and must have written terrible nonsense.

(The letter he refers to is missing, presumably destroyed at Curling's wish.)

I never left my tent at Helpmakar (sic) for fifteen days. The fever got better but I could not eat anything and was getting weaker every day, so they sent me down here in an ambulance, with a lot of other men and I began to feel better from the moment we left Helpmakar and I am all right now except being a little weak. It is a very bad fever and is accompanied by violent diarrea (sic).

Men were dying daily from it at Helpmakar (sic) and 60 out of 300 men were in hospital. The Company of Engineers had lost 9 men out of 120 and have half their number ill still.[11]

I am so sorry I wrote that stupid letter but I hardly knew what I was doing at the time.

I hope you are still quite well and find the climate agrees with you. I was so pleased to hear you got over the journey so well. Give my love to Papa: I am so ashamed of having written that stupid letter. The church is the hospital here and I am living with three other sick officers in the vestry. I have not written before as I have not been well enough.

By the end of March Curling was back at Helpmakaar and had resumed his normal duties.

1ˢᵗ April 1879 Helpmakar (sic) To Mama

I came up here from Ladysmith on Friday (28ᵗʰ) and I am strong enough to get about and do a little duty and another sub(altern) in my battery is away sick leaving only one to do all the duty. I find the change from a room with one's own bed etc and being able to undress rather trying. Up here, of course, I never take off my clothes except to wash and sleep on the ground as no such thing as a camp bed is to be had in Natal.

The duty is very trying, too: every other night I have to visit the sentries and guards after 12 and about every fourth night I am on fort duty and am up nearly all night.

We are only 3 miles from the Zulu border and after the way

in which our troops are being surprised we take every possible precaution. Even doing so, we should have a very poor chance should we be attacked at night by any large number of Zulus. Their spies are everywhere and we have little chance of getting any warning of attack.

Of course you have heard all about Col. Wood's fight. We, as yet, have had no particulars but our losses seem to have been very heavy. Poor Nicholson was one of the nicest fellows I ever met. He was in my room at the Academy and I have always known him well. He was heir to a baronetry. Barton, too, who was killed, has (£) 8 or 10,000 a year and only soldiered for pleasure.

Curling is obviously combining two battles; the assault on Hlobane on 28 March and the Zulu Attack on Wood's Encampment at Khambula on the 29 March.

After the disastrous attack on Hlobane mountain during which Captain Barton was killed, the Zulu impis continued their march on the camp at Khambula. Here they found a well-prepared defensive position and, despite their numerical superiority, they were kept at a distance by heavy rifle and artillery fire. The Zulus lost some 1,500 killed whereas the British sustained just twenty-six fatalities. One of these was Curling's friend, Frederick Nicholson of 11 Battery/7th Brigade.

The sickness here has decreased for the simple reason that there are not so many left to get ill. The weather is getting cooler so we hope that the worst is over. Nothing is known as to our ultimate destination: the remnant of the Centre Column seems to be forgotten by the General altogether. No doubt anything connected with it brings painful thoughts to him.

We expect it to be broken up and divided among the other columns. I have just received your letter with the news of your having heard of our troubles. I was not very anxious about your not hearing of my being all right, as I saw a copy of the telegram sent by the Special (*correspondent*) of the Standard (*F.R. MacKenzie*).

. . . This place is very depressing: what with the sickness, our heavy losses and the constant state of anxiety we are always in, it is difficult to be cheerful. It will be better when we move. We are all in for a far different business from what we expected. The Zulus seem to be able to get unlimited numbers of men and move in large masses. They are evidently recruited from tribes far distant from Zululand.

This was not so. The Zulus had suffered huge casualties at Isandlwana, Khambula and, shortly, Gingindlovu.

2nd April.

Our losses have been so very heavy. We have lost in action 1,400 white men out of 10,000 we began the war with and of the 12 Artillery officers in the Colony, 3 have already been killed . . . I ought to be promoted soon but look forward with fear to a bad fall as it is so difficult at this distance to make arrangements as to exchanging etc. When this war will be over, no one knows. After June it is impossible to do anything as there is no grass for the cattle and if it is not over by that time, we shall have to wait until next year.

4th April 1879 Helpmakar (sic) To Willy

I have answered your long letter but, having been seedy, must be excused. When I was ill, I wrote such a stupid letter: I think I must have been off my nut when I wrote it. I was laid up for six weeks altogether as it pulled one down terribly and the fever lasted three weeks.

I was sent down to a place called Ladysmith where there is a hospital and began to get better directly I left this (*Helpmakaar*). About 35 men and 2 officers have died of the fever which is a good proportion for a force of about 1000 men in the short space of two months.

All the men who die, the doctors say have typhoid and those who recover, intermittent fever. As about a quarter of the men have been sent away sick, there are not very many left who have not had it. The severe diarrea (sic) that everybody has with the fever is what pulls you down most. I could not walk a yard when I left there and lay on my back in an ambulance for three days going down to Ladysmith.

We are living a very hard life up here and the constant anxiety makes it very trying. We are living within three miles of the border and are constantly watched by Zulu spies.

The Fort is too small to sleep in and is too unhealthy, so we sleep in tents outside and are never quite safe from a surprise and the more so that the Zulus have been so successful in that form of attack. This is a very bloody war. Out of the 6,000 white men with which the General began the campaign, 1,500 have been killed or invalided from wounds. Out of the 12 Artillery officers in the Colony, 3 have been killed.

Col. Wood had a big fight which, although a success, shows the tremendous power of the Zulus. We shall see another 10,000 men out here before the war is over. We hope to move from this in about another two weeks and to advance again into Zululand in another month. But if things go on as they have been going lately, we shall not be strong enough to make any headway.

I do so long to come home and see you all again but it seems a terrible long way off. The worst of it is that I cannot get any credit out of it, only being a sub and one risks one's life without a chance of ever being thanked for it. This is a very selfish way of looking at things but really one gets tired of being a complete nonentity. . .We lost the whole of our field kit uniform etc at Isandlwana and wear most extraordinary clothes now: corduroy breeches etc. What I dislike most is sleeping on the ground, the constant rains have turned it quite into a bog and I am never a brilliant sleeper at any time. It is an advantage in one way that, what with visiting sentries, picquets and fort duty, one seldom gets a couple of hours sleep at a time.

We have got an awful lot of duffers out here on the staff: the only good man is Col. Wood and I am afraid he will be superceded by one of the Generals that have been sent out.

By the time you get this Papa and the others will be on their way home again I should think. May is quite a month to be in England.

119

*(Not that year, for 1879 holds the unenviable record for the greatest rainfall on record.)*

It was very good of you to wire to Cannes as they did not know till the next day who the killed were.

Our Columns now will not be at all strong: when the numerous sick and the garrisons of the numerous forts that have grown up as the border are deducted, each column will not number 4,000 men, too few to meet 20,000 or more of the enemy, elated as they are now by their success. I am afraid all this must be rather shop to you, but it is what we most think about.

Why does not Sir William Coghlan send Howard out here. He would get command of Native Cavalry at once and would not be able to get a drop of liquor once he got upcountry.[12]

7th April 1879 Helpmakar To Willy

Just received a large budget of letters including one from you dated Feb.22nd.

There is a runner starting in an hour with the mail so I have time to send you a few lines.

As soon as I am promoted, I shall be posted at once to some battery but shall not join it of course until the war is over. Should the battery be out of England, I may not see you again for years. I want a battery in England if possible and of course would prefer a Field Battery but hardly hope for such luck.

Will you thank Liz (*Willy's wife*) for her long letter and tell her I never got her photo. On the morning of the fight (*Isandlwana*), I got a photo of the Wedding but, of course, that with all the other photos, letters etc are all gone.

About kit, many thanks for your kind offer to send some out but I doubt whether it would ever reach me. Besides, we are not allowed to have tents and so our kit will be limited to a couple of blankets. We never undress now, except to wash.

I have a slight return of the fever; getting so little sleep had brought it on again, I think.

The men still continue to die from it. Seldom a day goes by without someone being buried.

I wonder if you will ever hear the true account about Isandlwana. We lost in killed 930 white men and 500 or more natives.

We leave this place on Thursday for a camp nearer Colonel Wood. Our Column will form one brigade of a force while Col. Wood will command the other brigade. He is far the best soldier out here and I wish we were joining with him.

Having been sent north to the new camp at Dundee, Curling was ordered to collect some reinforcements newly arrived from England.

28th April 1879 Victoria Club, Pietermaritzburg To Mama

I am living in luxury for a few days and enjoy it only as one who has been away in the wilds for five months. I have been sent here to bring up the 89 men that have been sent out from England to make up our losses at Isandlwana. I have to equip two guns with horses etc., and so expect to be here quite a week. I came down by post-cart from Dundee, the place where our new camp now is, about 25 miles from Helpmakar. We did 100 miles a day, starting at an hour before daylight and travelling until 9 or 10 at night. We changed horses every 10 or 12 miles and were nearly bumped to death over the bad roads.

I do so enjoy the change to a comfortable bed, dinner with table-cloth etc. Being alone, I put up at a hotel and can do what I like. Your letters all wrong: the last I got makes no mention of your having heard from me since Jan.22nd.

Of course, as long as I am away from Headquarters, I cannot get your letters but hope to get quite a budget when we get back. I see they have published the proceedings of the Court of Enquiry: when we were examined we had no idea this would be done and took no trouble to make a readable statement, at least one or two did so. It is two weeks march from this to the Frontier, but there is no chance of the troops advancing before we return. If the General delays more than a week or two, it will

121

be too late this year to do any good and we shall have to remain idle for five months.

The 17th Lancers marched away this morning: no one who had seen them in England would recognise them again.

Both the 17th Lancers and the King's Dragoon Guards were sent as reinforcements for the great losses the volunteer mounted regiments had sustained at Hlobane.

It is very amusing to read the accounts of Chard and Bromhead. They are about the most common-place men in the British Army. Chard is a most insignificant man in appearance and is only about 5 feet 2 or 3 in height. Bromhead is a stupid old fellow, as deaf as a post. Is it not curious how some men are forced into notoriety?

Both Chard and Bromhead were fêted in the press as the heroes of Rorke's Drift. Among their fellow officers, however, there was a certain amount of resentment and incredulity for their fame, as they did not fit the Victorian heroic image. Curling was not alone in disparaging Chard and Bromhead. Major Clery, a rather acerbic staff officer, wrote:

Well, Chard and Bromhead to begin with: both are almost typical in their separate corps of what would be termed the very dull class. Bromhead is a great favourite in his regiment and a capital fellow at everything except soldiering. So little was he held to be qualified in this way from unconquerable indolence that he had to be reported confidentially as hopeless. This is confidential, as I was told it by his commanding officer (Glyn) . . .

Chard there is very little to say about except that he too is a 'very good fellow' – but very uninteresting.

Chard's company commander, Walter Parke Jones, who had fortified Helpmakaar, was irritated by Chard's lack of ambition:

Chard makes me angry, with such a start as he got, he stuck to the company doing nothing. In his place, I should have gone up and asked Lord Chelmsford for an appointment, he must have got one, and if not he could have gone home soon after Rorke's Drift, at the height of his popularity at home. I advised him, but he placidly smokes his pipe and does nothing. Few men get such opportunities.

Chard was later attached to Colonel Wood's Column and he again failed to impress his superiors. Both Wood and Buller were puzzled that such a brilliant and stubborn defence had apparently been orchestrated by such mediocrity as Chard, 'A dull, heavy man, scarcely ever able to do his regular work'. Finally Sir Garnet Wolseley, who succeeded Lord Chelmsford, and who presented both Chard and Bromhead with their Victoria Crosses, was also critical. He found Chard, '. . . a hopelessly dull and stupid fellow, and Bromhead not much better'.

Despite adverse comments from their fellow officers, both Chard and Bromhead were favourably received by Queen Victoria. Unable or unwilling to take advantage of their fame and royal patronage, both men's careers did not prosper and both died before they were fifty.

## Notes

1. Sergeant R. Maxfield of 2/24th Regiment.
2. *The Red Soldier* by Frank Emery p. 133–4. Gunner Arthur Howard does not mention his remarkable escape in his letter. During the attack, he had helped to defend the loopholed hospital until it was set on fire and became untenable. From his position, he was unable to reach the safety of the barricades, so he made a dash for some nearby bushes and hid. Despite being surrounded by Zulus, he remained undetected until he emerged the next morning to the amazement of his comrades.
3. *The Zulu Campaign from a Military Point of View* by Lt. Col. Arthur Harness, *Fraser's Magazine*, May 1880, p. 477.
4. *Invasion of Zululand* by Sonia Clark, Brenthurst Press, 1979, p. 102.
5. *On the Psychology of Military Incompetence* by Norman Dixon, Cape, 1976.
6. Colonel Charles Fairfax Hassard acted as Cetshwayo's gaoler when the Zulu chief was held captive at Cape Town.
7. Army Historical Research, Vol. 59, Spring 1981, p. 47.

8 Ibid. N Battery, 5th Brigade, Royal Artillery at Isandlwana, 22 January 1879 by Major P.E. Abbott, RA.(ret), FRSA, FSAScot.
9 *The Invasion of Zululand* by Sonia Clark, ibid, p. 92.
10 The hospital and all its supplies had been destroyed at Rorke's Drift so there was an almost total lack of medicines and equipment to treat the sick.
11 *The Invasion of Zululand* by Sonia Clark, ibid, p. 102.
12 Sir William Coughlan was the author of the letter of introduction that Curling carried for so long and never presented. Presumably, the cryptic remark refers to a wayward son of Coughlan's.

# Chapter Eight

# Chelmsford's Revenge

Lord Chelmsford sought to salvage his battered reputation by guarding the border with Zululand and amassing a large force for a second invasion. He saw his first priority as the relief of Colonel Pearson's Coastal Column, which had been besieged at the mission of Eshowe.

Having crossed into Zululand near where the Tugela River met the Indian Ocean it took from 18–23 January to cover the thirty odd miles to reach the hilltop station at Eshowe. During this hard march, which reduced their route to a broad ribbon of mud, Pearson's men fought the first battle of the War. On the morning of 22 January, by the Inyezane River, some 6,000 Zulus attacked Pearson's vanguard. In a sharp battle that lasted ninety minutes, the British repulsed the attack by quickly bringing into action an extended firing line, rockets and, for the first time in a land battle, a Gatling gun. The Battle of Inyzane preceded Isandlwana by a few hours but its modest victory was overshadowed by the catastrophe of the latter.

Pearson reached Eshowe and immediately set to building an impressive fort. When news of Chelmsford's defeat reached Pearson, he called a council of war among his more senior officers to decide whether to retreat to Natal or stay put. The majority chose to stay and so began three months of misery, hunger and sickness for the defenders. The Zulus kept a minimum presence, enough to dissuade Pearson from evacuating his fortress.

Meanwhile, Chelmsford began to receive the first of the reinforcements; within a matter of weeks he felt strong enough to attempt to relieve Pearson. On 28 March over 5,000 men of the Eshowe Relief Column crossed the Tugela and trudged through the rain-sodden country. Chelmsford, having learned his lesson, ordered that each stopping place should be laagered and entrenched. This precaution paid dividends for, on the morning of 2 April and within sight of Eshowe, Chelmsford's encampment was attacked near the old military kraal of Gingindlovu. In a battle that lasted just ninety minutes, the Zulus were routed and sustained about 1,200 killed.

The following morning Eshowe was relieved. As Pearson's sickly command left with the Relief Column, they left behind twenty-five of their comrades buried in the tiny cemetery.

Having returned to Natal, Chelmsford was now able to concentrate on his preparations for the Second Invasion.

Curling continues in his letter dated 28 April:

I am sorry to say our column is still to be commanded by the General (*Lord Chelmsford*). I think these disasters have quite upset his judgement or rather that of his staff and one does not feel half so comfortable under his command as with a man like Col. Wood. Our Column is nearly certain to be the one that will have all the fighting.

The Zulus are afraid of Col. Wood with his veteran regiments. Our force is entirely composed of young troops who have no experience of fighting and one trembles to think how easily a panic might occur.

The reinforcements sent consisted almost entirely of raw recruits. The Infantry Brigade was made up of the newly reconstructed 1/24th and the 2/21st, 58th and 94th Regiments. In the event, they all behaved steadily in the final battle at Ulundi, although en route there had been incidents of panic. During one night, sentries opened fire on a returning patrol, which in turn fired back. The camp thought they were under attack, tents were collapsed and the infantry blazed away into the African night. Melton Prior, the Special for the *Illustrated London News,* wrote in his memoirs, ' A more disgraceful scene I have never witnessed, more particularly when one realised that six rounds of canister were actually fired by the artillery, without having seen a single enemy'.[1]

Such was the desire to show the British in a good light, the news reporters present exercised a self-censorship and this and several similar incidents went unreported. Arthur Harness wrote of this incident, 'None of my guns were fired, I am glad to say, but the confusion and random firing was terrible.' His battery's tents and equipment were riddled with bullets, two horses were killed and five men wounded.[2] Curling also wrote, '. . . It is amusing what a crowd of outsiders have come out here. Parsons, photographers, newspaper people by dozens and no end of loafers. I fancy but few of them will ever get farther than this town where they can write lies to people at home as well as anywhere else'.

Curling was being unfair to the press contingent, which were determined to report the war from the front and had to overcome Chelmsford's efforts to have them excluded from the Column. By not ingratiating himself with the visiting newsmen, Chelmsford invited hostility and criticism, which he received in abundance.

28th May 1879 Landman's Drift To Mama

Just a few lines to say that I am in perfect health, indeed I have never been stronger.

You will see all about our doings in the papers as there are (sic) an army of correspondents out here now.

I went with the Cavalry Brigade to Isandlwana and on the following day assisted to bury Maj. Smith, but you will see full accounts of everything in the papers . . . I have been so constantly on the move lately that I have had no time to write and all patrolls (sic) now are made without tents so one cannot write in the open air.

I found my account book and several letters etc at Isandlwana but no vestige of the despatch box.

On 21 May Curling found himself back at Rorke's Drift as part of General Marshall's force sent to bury the dead at Isandlwana and to salvage any usable equipment. It was an all-mounted party consisting of the newly arrived 17th Lancers and the King's Dragoon

Guards, four volunteer units and two guns of Curling's Battery commanded by Colonel Harness. They crossed the Buffalo River before light and cautiously approached the battlefield. The sight that met them was a melancholy one. Both Melton Prior and Archibald Forbes of the *Daily News* were on hand to record the scene, which they both described graphically. Prior wrote, 'The sight I saw at Isandlwana is one I shall never forget. In all the seven campaigns I have been in . . . I have never witnessed a scene more horrible. I have seen dead and dying on a battle-field by hundreds and thousands; but to come to a spot where the slaughtered battalion of the 24th Regiment and others were lying at Isandlwana, was far more appalling. Here I saw not the bodies but the skeletons of men I had known in life and health, some of whom I had known well, mixed up with the skeletons of oxen and horses, and with wagons thrown on their side, all in great confusion, showing how furious had been the onslaught of the enemy'.

Forbes wrote, '. . . All the way up the slope I traced by the ghastly token of dead men, the fitful line of flight. Most of the men hereabouts were infantry of the 24th. It was like a long string with knots in it, the string formed of single corpses, the knots clusters of dead, where (as it seemed) little groups might have gathered to make a hopeless, gallant stand and die.

I came upon a gully with a gun limber jammed on its edge, and the horses, their hides scored with assegai stabs, hanging in their harness down the steep face of the ravine . . .'

Forbes report gave the erroneous impression that the gun-limber had toppled into a ravine. What in fact happened was that the ground for the first half a mile was quite smooth and the two gun teams made good progress until they tried to cross the rocky bed of a dried donga that crossed the floor of the ravine. It was here that the guns possibly became stuck and the gunners and horses were killed.

Curling's letter beginning Page 2 (1st page missing):

I told you that when we visited Isandlwana we found the gun limber which was more particularly in my charge just where I left it. The horses were lying dead in their harness and the drivers a few paces off. Of the other gun and horses, there was no trace.

Curling and his men buried their dead comrades as they found them. (The cairns have been examined and, along with the skeletons, Royal Artillery uniform buttons found). The two guns had been dragged away and were regarded purely as trophies by the Zulus, who had no idea how to operate them.

> The dead are now nearly all buried and in a few days the grass which is 5 or 6 feet high is to be set on fire when all traces of the fight will be erased. We find all sorts of articles taken from Isandlwana all over the country, every kraal has something: the stock of a fishing rod I had was found a few days ago and something is brought in every day.

A previous patrol had travelled the trail of the fugitives and found Major Smith's body. Because of the remoteness of the area, it was decided to reach it by crossing the river at the Fugitive's Drift; the river was now low and gently flowing. The following day, 22 May Colonel Harness crossed the river with Curling and his battery, leaving a squadron of lancers to guard the crossing. Harness wrote to his sister:

> Some two hundred yards up, we found poor Stuart Smith's remains and we dug a grave. One of us read a service and marked the place with stones and a wooden cross. Melton Prior was with us and he took four sketches, so you will see them in the *Illustrated London News*. We also buried another artillery man we found.

Unfortunately, Prior's sketches were not published. It is possible they were among the portfolio of sketches he lost during the Battle of Ulundi and which have never come to light.

7th June 1879 With Lord Chelmsford's Column, Ityotzozi River, Zululand To Mama

We are now well into Zululand and far farther in than any of the Columns have been before. I only hope that we shall have a fight soon before we get farther into the country.

We get more careless everyday and one trembles to think of what would happen should we be attacked at night. Our arrangements on the march are pretty good and the worst that could happen would be to lose a part of our baggage but at night we are shut up in a huge entrenchment half a mile long, far too large for us to defend properly. The natives retreat before us, fighting us as they go.

You have heard, of course, all about the poor little Prince Imperial's death and yesterday, the Adjutant of the 17th Lancers (*Lieutenant John Cokayne Frith*) was killed in a skirmish in which I believe the enemy suffered no loss.

. . . I was one of the pall-bearers at the Prince's funeral: poor little fellow, everyone feels so sorry for him and ashamed that he should meet his death in such a way.

The day after the Second Invasion got underway, yet another disaster occurred. Lord Chelmsford's painstaking preparations and precautions had not taken into consideration the vanity and recklessness of the heir to the French throne, Louis Napoleon, the Prince Imperial. Like Curling, the Prince had graduated as an artillery officer, although he was not eligible to serve in the British Army. Anxious to test his courage, he badgered the War Office until he was allowed to travel to South Africa and join a reluctant Chelmsford as an extra aide. There had been episodes when the Prince had galloped off alone after Zulus when attached to Buller's command. The latter refused to take responsibility for the Prince, which had resulted in Louis being confined to camp duties.

Thinking that he would be in no danger, Chelmsford's staff allowed the Prince to ride out with a six-man escort and another officer, named Lieutenant Carey, to look for a suitable campsite for the following day. At the Prince's insistence, they had descended into a wide valley and stopped for a rest by an abandoned kraal. Just as they prepared to mount up and resume their patrol, a Zulu scouting party who had approached through the long grass attacked them. It happened so quickly that there was no time to offer any resistance and it was every man for himself as they pulled themselves onto their horses and spurred away. Two troopers were quickly shot and killed before they could mount. Louis's horse was panicked by the com-

130

motion and took off with the Prince desperately clinging onto the holster attached to his saddle. After 150 yards, the strap broke and Louis went sprawling. In an instant, the Zulus were upon the prince and stabbed him to death.

The next morning a search party retrieved his body. A service was read in the camp and the body was placed on Curling's gun carriage and carried around the assembled parade. The pallbearers were Captains R. Alexander and F. Vibart, and Lieutenants J. Wodehouse, E.H. Elliot, C.S.B. Parsons and Henry Curling. The next morning, the body was taken back to the base camp at Landsman's Drift and from there, it was conveyed by relays until it was returned by sea to England. The Prince Imperial's death provoked an enormous amount of press coverage and the impact on the British public was even greater than that of Isandlwana. The main reason was that the special correspondents were in camp and the story received great attention, which was out of proportion to its importance.

No one knows where the Zulu Army is and until it has been defeated we are in a very ticklish position. I wish I could tell you all I think about it but don't like to do so in a letter . . . We do not seem to profit from our experience, Our baggage columns are larger than ever and we carry tents, camp-beds etc., just the same as before. None of the troops from England believe in the enemy and we old stagers are called alarmists.

You would hardly believe it possible but we do not know the road and are wandering on with the greatest uncertainty as to where we shall go.

. . . Col. Wood's Column marches a few miles ahead of us. It is a pity we are not organised like him but we consist of Generals with large staffs: too many cooks spoil the pudding and we have no less than five generals (including two Brigadiers) with us. We are having lovely weather and are making the most of the short season before all the grass is burnt.

Whether we shall finish the war remains to be seen but there can be no real peace until the Zulus have been thoroughly beaten and their cattle taken. The conditions of peace are very mild and there is some little chance of the Zulu King giving in to save himself. We cannot be certain that his chiefs will agree with him and everything will remain in a most dangerous state. I am wonderfully strong now, can sleep anywhere, at anytime and eat anything.

Arthur Harness also commented on the top-heavy nature of the Staff, 'There is also a tremendous staff: all Lord Chelmsford's and General Newdigate's . . . Indeed the whole thing has taken such large proportions that it makes one rather sad and wish for the old days when two or at most three tents formed the headquarters camp; now it is as large as a regiment.'

Lord Chelmsford proceeded at a snail's pace towards Ulundi, covering about 100 miles in four weeks.

Curling's parents had allowed the letter describing their son's escape to be published in *The Standard* on 27 March, which included the offending sentence, 'Most of those who escaped were volunteers and native contingent officers who tell any number of lies.' Once this became known back in Natal, it sparked a minor diplomatic incident, which involved Curling's commanding officer, Colonel Harness. He referred to it in his next letter:

> I had no end of trouble about that letter that was put into *The Standard* and have been freely abused in the local papers for the remarks about the Volunteers. After all, letters are dangerous things to write freely as one is not certain who may see them. There was nothing untrue in my letter and yet what trouble it has got me in.

Harness wrote a letter to his sister Caroline from Landman's Drift Camp on 24 May 1879:

> . . . I think I told you of one of my subaltern's letters to his mother being published in *The Standard* some time ago. His letter, which comments most unwarrantedly on the conduct of the volunteer officers and officers of native contingents, calling them all 'liars' etc., has been copied into the colonial papers and the result is that I have had to advise him to write an apology. I do not see what else he could do. Is it not too stupid of his people to put such a thing in print?

132

Shepstone, who commands the volunteers, came to me and said his men thought it the unkindest cut of all that my battery, which had been such friends, and that all had liked so much, should abuse them in that way. I could only say that what a man writes to his wife or mother, he could hardly dream would be in print and that it was written under excitement etc, etc, and that he was very sorry etc.[3]

Once again, Curling seems to have incurred Harness's displeasure and promotion seemed ever distant. It may have been this incident that prompted Harness to leave Curling at Fort Marshall, one of the strong points built to guard the route to Ulundi.

30th June 1879 Fort Marshall, Zululand To Mama

We are quite out of it here from any news of what is going on and never get any letters as the mail bags go on direct to Headquarters and no one takes the trouble to send our letters back. There is one consolation, in another 10 days their provisions will all be gone so they must return when, I hope, we shall all go back to Natal. All our jams, tinned things etc., are all gone and we live entirely on rations and in fact are quite grateful for a discovery we made that Enos Fruit Salt is a capital substitute for baking powder in making bread. Now that the Fort is nearly finished there is little to occupy the men with and we all find it very monotonous. Every morning, we stand to our arms from 5 am until daylight, which is not until 6.30 and you can understand how pleasant that is in these frosty mornings.

Our latest news of the General is that he is starting with a flying column this day for Ulundi, from which he is now only about 10 miles distant but the country is difficult and dangerous so that he can only move slowly. A special messenger from Sir Garnet Wolseley arrived yesterday with a long telegram for Lord Chelmsford. We all fancy that peace will be made at any price. The King has already sent 200 oxen and some ivory as a peace offering but the guns do not come and they are to be the first signs that he really means not to fight.

Because of the Isandlwana disaster and the general mishandling of the campaign, Lord Chelmsford was relieved of his command and replaced by General Sir Garnet Wolseley, regarded as the best soldier of his day. Due to the length of time it had taken to reach South Africa and then the frustrations of physically taking command of the army in the field, Wolseley did not take over until Chelmsford achieved his victory at Ulundi. Curling continued:

I met (*Captain*) Fred Campbell of the 94th a few days ago. I suppose I knew him as a boy a long time ago. He wished to be remembered to you and Papa.

I passed through Escourt on the road from Maritzburg but not then knowing that Fred Birkett was living near there, did not enquire about him. I met a cousin of his in the Native Contingent: he is anything but a nice fellow. Emmy's friend's cousin, Captain (Bindon) Blood is with the Lower Column, a very long way from this.

What a block there is on promotion just now, only four steps since Jan 22nd, when poor Smith was killed.

I could not help thinking when we were burying him, how nearly I shared the same fate. He did not appear to be assegaied and most probably died from the effects of falling down the rocks. We found his horse dead a little above him and 19 other white men who had all either fallen or been shot down while climbing the rocks.

. . . Your letters, when they come, are most cheerful and pleasant: what great travellers you have all become. Papa will never be satisfied with Ramsgate after this. I long to see the place again and shall be quite heartbroken if I get promoted to a battery out here or, what is worse, in Mauritius or St. Helena.

Nearly all the Captains in these batteries have been sent out for the war and return home as soon as it is over so it will simplify matters very much to promote me to one of their vacancies . . . We all think it very probable that the Battery will be ordered home as soon as the war is over and it quite possible that I may be promoted before and may come with it. Would it not be pleasant? We hear that the remainder of the Battery has been stopped at another fort, so it matters little which fort you remain in if you are stuck in one at all.

Fort Marshall was built and garrisoned on 18 June by two companies of 2/21st Regiment. Two troops of 17th Lancers were based there and patrolled the area. Captain F.M.E. Vibart commanded the two guns that had been sent out as replacements for those lost at Isandlwana. The Fort consisted of two joined pentagons, roughly 130 metres in length by 30 metres wide. The defences were little more than a shallow ditch with earth and stone battlements.

5th July 1879 Fort Marshall To Mama

We heard this morning of yesterday's battle. Forbes, the correspondent, got here at daylight having ridden all night through a dangerous country. He hopes to get to the end of the wire about 50 miles off this evening: anyhow, he is far ahead of all the other correspondents.

He is a great, strong, coarse-looking man, able to undergo any amount of fatigue and to put up with any amount of snubbing. These Specials are a terrible nuisance. They expect to be welcomed everywhere and in fact come whether you welcome them or not. One feels at the same time that it is dangerous to be uncivil to them. They are obliged to be pushing, unsnubbable men, no others would get on at all.

Archibald Forbes was the most influential war correspondent of his day. His highly descriptive and punchy prose, together with his determination to be first with the news, made him the natural successor to the great William Russell. Forbes was a superb horseman, having been trained as a trooper in the Royal Dragoons, and possessed great stamina. His career lasted no more than ten years but in that time he changed the way wars were reported.

In the Zulu War he was very critical of Lord Chelmsford and hounded him long after the war was over. Having stood in the British square at Ulundi and watched the destruction of Cetshwayo's army, Forbes was anxious to send off his account with the first courier taking news of the victory to the telegraph at Landman's Drift. With

135

the countryside full of scattered bands of Zulus, Chelmsford prudently thought it too dangerous to send a messenger. Scornful of the General, Forbes blurted out, 'Then, sir, I will start myself at once'. Afterwards he admitted, 'I was sorry for myself the moment I had spoken'. In a generous act, Forbes took Melton Prior's sketches as well as some staff messages.

Leaving at dusk, Forbes carefully followed the wagon tracks, frequently stopping to hide from dark figures of Zulus he saw by the light of blazing kraals. Once he was clear of the area around Ulundi, Forbes made good progress, changing horses six times, including at Fort Marshall. At about 3p.m. the following day, an exhausted Forbes reached Landman's Drift having travelled 120 miles in twenty hours.

The telegraph had been extended to the Cape so news now reached London in twenty-four hours.

Having sent his report, Forbes then rode on to Durban, where he mailed his full story and Prior's sketches. Incredibly he had travelled 295 miles in just fifty-five hours!

Forbes' report was the first to reach Britain and was read out in both Houses of Parliament. It bought him even greater fame and his exploit came to be known as 'The Ride of Death', and there was even a media suggestion that he should receive the Victoria Cross. In the event, Lord Chelmsford even blocked Forbes's claim for a campaign medal, which was not the wisest act. Angered by this, Forbes conducted a campaign in print to have Chelmsford held accountable for the incompetent way the war had been conducted. In this, he was only partially successful for, although Chelmsford never again held a field command, his peers showered him with honours. An exhausted and disillusioned Archibald Forbes retired from reporting and concentrated his remaining twenty years on lecturing and writing books.[4]

Curling continues:

How pluckily the Zulus still fight: they are apparently unable to get large armies together now. From the 22,000 that attacked Col. Wood at Kambula (sic) 100 miles from the Chief Kraal Ulundi, they dwindled down to 10,000 or even less that attacked yesterday near the Kraal itself. From the top of a mountain close to us, we saw Ulundi in flames but it was not till this morning that we heard of the fight that our people had.

# Chelmsford's Revenge

Lord Chelmsford can now resign most peacefully and we all expect him to do so as soon as he can hand the command over to Sir Garnet Woolsy (sic). He has not an easy job before him, I think. The country is getting blacker every day and there is now hardly a blade of grass in our line of communications; all has been burnt. Sir Garnet will have to get the Army back with its 10,000 men and 600 wagons and he is dealing with an enemy who apparently will not make peace but will fight to the end.

We have now done nearly all the harm in country that we can. All the open country has been overrun, the kraals burnt and the crops destroyed. We cannot get the cattle: they have been driven into an inaccessible country far out of reach.

I suppose we need not fear the Zulus attacking us in any considerable force unless they can get us at a disadvantage, but still it will be interesting to see the result.

After four weeks of slow progress, Chelmsford's Column formed a huge square on the plain at Ulundi. It took less than half an hour of concentrated Martini-Henry, Gatling and artillery fire to break the Zulus' spirit. Even in defeat, they made a stirring sight as they chanted and rattled their assegais against their stiff cowhide shields before swishing through the grass in a charge to their destruction.

Curling's Battery was represented by just two guns under the command of Colonel Harness who wrote of the battle:

The guns opened fire on the enemy at about two thousand yards or more, from all four sides, and the Zulus came on pluckily in small groups taking wonderful advantage of cover. But our fire was tremendous, as you can imagine, and after half an hour or so they regularly turned and bolted; then the lancers and other mounted men went out with a cheer from us and I believe did their work well, but Drury Lowe told me their horses were a good deal pumped. The Zulus ran so fast they had a considerable distance to go before they got to the scattered retreat of the enemy. In the rear face of the square the enemy got to within forty yards. On my own side, the left face, they did not come within four hundred yards I should say, but my two seven-pounders made excellent shooting.[5]

137

With British pride restored and Chelmsford able to resign with some credit, the Column withdrew to Fort Marshall, where it was broken up on 27 July. Most marched down to Durban, where they embarked for Britain, while the rest, including Curling's Battery, were formed into two flying columns. Curling's column was commanded by Lieutenant Colonel Baker Creed Russell, 13th Hussars, one of Wolseley's 'Gang'. A veteran of the Indian Mutiny and the Ashanti War, Russell was regarded as a very able and energetic officer. He took his column, called the Baker Russell column, and proceeded to the north-west in a sweep that searched for the fugitive King Cetshwayo. Along the way, Curling was able to write a letter from Fort Cambridge, about twenty miles south of Hlobane:

5th August 1879 Fort Cambridge, Zululand To Mama

We have had a move since I last wrote and are in quite a different part of Zululand about 40 miles from my old station, Fort Marshall. We form part of a small column under Col. Baker-Russell, who seems to be a smart, go-ahead man, though of course he knows nothing about the style of fighting out here as yet.

We have been marching for the last three days and halted today to give the cattle a rest. Tomorrow, we move on again into a country where we have never been before, leaving a small forti-fied post here.

Zululand is now covered with little forts which are useful in preventing Zulus from returning to their kraals without our knowledge. When they come back and give up their arms, they will bring their cattle which will be a good security for their future behaviour. The Zulu King has still some 10,000 men who will follow him. They are all young men who own no cattle or wives and who have nothing to lose if they are beaten, so there is a good chance of our having another fight. Anyhow, another week will show whether the campaign is over or not. I am so glad to get out of the fort and thoroughly enjoy being on the move again. I dined with Fred Campbell last night: he was sent up with some troops to make the fort here a few days ago. I have not heard from you now for a long time: your last letter was

138

written just after arriving at Ramsgate. The changes in the different Divisions have quite upset all postal arrangements and our letters are flying about all over the country.

Sir Garnet's protégés have completely taken charge of everything out here and the whole of the old staff have been shipped back to England. Many of them have been but a month or two out here.

We shall have some terrible disaster some day caused by the newspapers and Members of Parliament trying to govern armies in the field. It will be quite impossible to keep up discipline now that flogging is done away with. However, it will soon be established again as men will now have occasionally to be shot and then what an outcry there will be.

Curling took a traditional army view on the question of flogging as a means of maintaining discipline in the field and added a rather extreme theory of his own. During the period of the War, no less than 545 British soldiers were flogged; the highest number in one year for many years. The wrongdoer was usually given twenty-five lashes for offences ranging from drunkenness and stealing to insubordination and desertion. A common offence was 'dereliction of duty', which covered those sentries who fell asleep when on guard duty, and merited fifty lashes. Once the increase in flogging became known in Britain, there was an outcry against this barbaric punishment, especially as it had been used on young recruits, and this led to it being banned.

12th August 1879 Emlongana Mifuni Station, Zululand To Mama

We have been on the move almost continuously since I last wrote. Col. Baker Russell, who commands this column, seems inclined to be far more energetic than the commanders we have been under before.

Finding that our guns cannot get over the country, he has turned us into cavalry and I returned last night from a three days patrol (sic) right through the most difficult part of Zululand. We heard that the Zulu King was hiding in a kraal about 50 miles

139

off, so Baker Russell took out the whole of the cavalry, about 400 strong, to try and catch him.

We started at daybreak three days ago taking nothing with us but some preserved meat and biscuit in our haversacks and went right into the heart of Zululand. The country was covered with Zulus who ran up into the mountains as we advanced. If they had chosen, they could have cut us all off as, in crossing the mountains, we had to go through numerous places in single file leading our horses. However, they only fired at us once and nobody was hit. When we had gone about 30 miles, the horses were too done up to go on, so we reluctantly turned back. As it was, we had to leave about 50 horses behind us and many men came back on foot. We slept at night with nothing but our great-coats on and our saddles for pillows and as we were in the saddle from daylight till dark for three days, were pretty done up when we returned last night. We can never drive the Zulus out of the mountains; at any rate, it will take years to do so and I have no wish to have to assist in doing it. I think Sir Garnet is too sensible to allow the war to drag on. If we had only been allowed to fight in the proper way, the war would have been over now. After the action at Ulundi we might have burnt most of the kraals and taken any number of cattle besides killing plenty of Zulus but we did nothing and reaped no benefit from our victory.

I shall not know what to do when I get home; it will take some to get civilised. It is now nearly seven months since I have slept without my clothes and boots except a couple of weeks at Ladysmith when I was sick. There seems but little chance of our going home and still less of being promoted. I almost despair of seeing you again. There will be two vacancies very shortly in batteries out here and it will be so very convenient to promote me to one of them unless I can get some kind friend to put in a word for me.

The two guns taken from Isandlwana were found abandoned just six miles from Ulundi. They were taken to Durban and put on display in a shed at Pine Terrace, where they proved to be a big attraction with the public. The missing limber was found with them and, upon inspection, they were declared undamaged. The Zulus had made an unsuccessful attempt to fire them using rifle percussion caps.[6] Colonel Harness was asked what he wanted done with the guns, which represented too many bad memories for him, so he said, 'Send them home – so they are going home. I thought it best to say so, although I have really not much feeling in the matter'.[7]

8th September 1879 Luneburg To Mama

Your letters are beginning to arrive with great regularity as the Post Office people have found out that we belong to Baker Russell Column. Unfortunately we heard this morning that the column is to be broken up and we start for Utrecht tomorrow morning.

When we arrive at Utrecht we shall either be ordered to Pretoria or Pietermaritzburg: we hope the latter but probably the Battery will be divided. Col. Harness has gone down to Maritzburg on leave and hopes to get leave home at once. As soon as we are settled I think I shall put in for leave too, if I don't get some steps in the meantime. The Zulu War is now completely over and the natives are most friendly. The Border tribes are the only ones that give any trouble. We are now encamped close to the spot where Captain Moriarty's Company was destroyed and have found the skeletons of several men who were killed while trying to escape.

Curling refers to the attack at Intombe Drift on the morning of 12 March. A Company of the 80th (The Staffordshire Volunteers) Regiment had been sent out from Luneburg to bring in a convoy of supply wagons, which had been delayed by the muddy road and the swollen Intombe River. Unable to complete the crossing before nightfall, Captain Moriarty was compelled to form a laager on the northern bank, while a small section made camp on the south bank.

About 5 a.m. as the mist began to lift, there was volley fired into the slumbering camp and 900 warriors charged in amongst the unprepared soldiers. Moriarty managed to get off three shots before being stabbed to death. The slaughter was swift but some soldiers managed to swim the narrow river and join their comrades on the south bank. Lieutenant Harward directed a covering fire until it was noticed that about 200 Zulus were crossing the river and attempting the encircle them. Pausing only to order Sergeant Anthony Booth to fall back on a farmhouse three miles to the rear, Harward mounted his horse and galloped off to Luneburg to raise the alarm. Most of his men and a few escapees followed him.

Booth was left with just eight men and a few escapees, who armed themselves. Calmly forming them into a square formation, Booth and his small band managed to keep the Zulus at a distance with volley fire as they slowly retreated. By the time they reached the deserted farmhouse, the Zulus had given up and returned to plunder the camp.

For his bravery and calmness, Booth was justly awarded the Victoria Cross. Lieutenant Harward, on the other hand, was court martialled for abandoning his men under fire. Somehow he managed to convince the court of his innocence and he was acquitted of the charge. Sir Garnet Wolseley was furious but could not change the Court's ruling. Instead, he let his feeling be known in a General Order that was read out to every regiment. With his career and reputation in tatters, Harward had little option but to resign.

Curling continues:

There is a small tribe here living in some caves in a mountain that overlooks the road, who will not submit. They have continued to fire on everybody passing by and have prevented any small parties from moving about. The first day we came here we surrounded their caves and summoned them to surrender. 8 of them came out with their arms and gave themselves up. Unfortunately some of our men were fired upon from another cave and our own niggers immediately assegaied the prisoners. The others then refused to come out. Large fires were lit at the mouth of the cave to smoke them out, but without avail.

We have been here 3 days and they will not give in so, as we move tomorrow and this nest of . . . (?) cannot be left here, the caves are to be blown up with gun-cotton. We are expecting to hear the explosion every minute. It seems cruel but must be done. The climate is getting as it always does just before the rains – very oppressive.

# Chelmsford's Revenge

These recalcitrant natives were the remnants of Mbilini's band who, although small in numbers, were still able to disrupt military traffic passing along the Luneburg to Lynchburg road. The blowing up of their caves ended all hostilities and the Zulu War was finally ended.

## Notes

1  *Campaigns of a War Correspondent* by Melton Prior.
2  *Invasion of Zululand* by Sonia Clark, Brenthurst Press, 1979, p. 135.
3  Ibid p. 127.
4  *AZWHS*, December 1999, p. 18.
5  *Invasion of Zululand* by Sonia Clark, ibid, p. 149.
6  *Natal Mercury*, 18 September 1879.
7  *Invasion of Zululand* by Sonia Clark, ibid, p. 176.

# Chapter Nine

# Afghanistan and Departures

With the War concluded, Curling fully expected to be sent home and to gain his captaincy. Once again, despite promotion, he was to be disappointed and destined to spend a further three frustrating months in the Transvaal, a country anxious to be rid of British occupation.

24th September 1879 Wesselstrom To Mama

I am quietly settled down in this little out of the way place and hope to remain here until I get orders to go home or to some place via England. You will find this village marked on the map as quite a large place but it only contains about 6 houses. It is, however, quite a large town for the Transvaal.

The rainy season has set in and it is poor for travelling and you cannot make certain of going even a few miles in a day. The remainder of the Battery has gone to Heidelburg en route for Pretoria but I hope not to be ordered to follow them but to remain here for the next two or three weeks at least.

Fortunately we are nearly all starving so until supplies are sent up, we cannot move. We hear that there are some young Subs on their way out to replace me and Fowler but I rather fear that they will not allow one of them to replace me in command of a detachment. The end of November ought to see me in England, at least I hope so. I should like very much to be with you and Papa in the South of France for a short time. How jolly it will be if we spend Christmas all together again this year. As Emmy says, if I don't look sharp, home will be so changed I shall not know it.

The next letter brings the first news of Curling's long awaited promotion, something which he receives with less than enthusiasm:

2nd October 1879 Wesselstrom, Transvaal To Mama

Two of your long letters arrived yesterday: as usual they made a trip up to Pretoria where the headquarters of the Battery are, and so arrived a week later than they should have done. However, they brought the first news of my promotion. I ought to feel very glad but I don't feel so, as our meeting again seems a long way off. I should so have liked to have been with you for the wedding: they will all have so many fresh ties that I shall be quite out of it when I come home.

During Curling's service in South Africa, his brother and two sisters, were married. Curling's letter continues:

'Papa was very kind in taking so much trouble about my promotion. He was successful, too, as the very good fall I have got shows.'

8th November, 1879 Wesselstrom To Mama

I received a letter from you dated Oct.4th, three days ago, by far the quickest delivery we have ever had. There are three mails still missing and the last letter I got was dated September 8th, so you can see how badly managed our postal arrangements are.

I can hear nothing of my getting away. Col. Law evidently intends to keep me as long as he can. I fear very much that I shall lose the battery to which I am promoted as a battery in active service must have all its officers with it. It is one comfort that

146

I never could have got up for the march on Carbul (sic) through in time to earn another medal. I don't think I am strong enough for a long campaign in a hot climate, so it may turn out for the best that I have not been able to get away. We are all very weak now and sickly. I suppose it comes from the fatigues of the campaign that has just finished and from the bad food which is worse now than it has ever been. I have not tasted any fresh vegetables, not even potatoes, fresh milk or butter for six months and the bread we get is bad and made of Indian corn flower (sic). My detachment consists of 50 men: ten of these are in hospital and one died a few days ago. Fever is the general complaint and it comes from having no protection from the intense heat of the sun.

If eventually they send me to join by way of England, I shall be able to see you all and, should the campaign have terminated, get leave until the last troopship leaves in April which will give plenty of time to make any arrangements. If, on the other hand, there is fighting still going on, I shall come in for another medal and eventually so much service ought to do me good.

There is nothing to tell you about this country. The local papers are full of rumours about the Boer fighting but I believe all these reports are only got up to keep the troops in the country as they spend no end of money. I am afraid my last letter was rather dismal but I was much depressed at being kept here doing nothing, when my (new) battery was fighting and everybody who had been a few months out here, going home.

Curling was appointed Captain in C Battery, 3rd Brigade, which was already involved in the war in Afghanistan and was marching with General Roberts to capture the capital, Kabul.

The reports of Boer unrest that Curling dismissed as a ruse to keep British troops in the Transvaal and support the local economy, were, in fact, true. Very shortly, the Boers inflicted a series of humiliating defeats on the British in a brief conflict known as the First Boer War. The most damaging defeat was at Majuba Hill, where Wolseley's replacement, Sir George Colley, was killed. The N/5 remained in the Transvaal and so participated in their third war in as many years.

147

## The Curling Letters of the Zulu War

26th November 1879 Pretoria, Transvaal To Mama

Your letters all go astray now. I have been moving about so much lately that they are following me about all over the country. I seem to get farther away from home instead of nearer. This place is 500 miles from the sea and the whole journey is made by road except about 30 miles of rail. I quite despair of ever getting out of the country.

We are close to the Tropics now and find the heat almost unsupportable, the Transvaal is a most hideous country, perfectly flat and uninhabited. You go for 30 miles and don't see any people, house, water or even cattle. We took a fortnight in marching up here from Wesselstroom and it was a great surprise when we arrived here to see such a civilised and pretty little town. On the road there were no inns, people who travel have to take their own tents and food. The post cart travels day and night and yet takes a week to get to Durban. I forget whether I told you that the Captain of the Battery has shammed sick and gone down to Maritzburg, leaving me in command of the Battery. He has nothing the matter with him really, only has managed to get up an attack of gout and drinking large quantities of beer. The real reason is that he wants to get home to his wife and family but is very hard to keep one to do his duty. The accounts and everything connected with the Battery are in the greatest state of confusion. I have refused to have anything to do with the payment and I don't know how things will go on.

Curling refers to the corpulent (fifteen stone) Captain Vibart, who had previously incurred Arthur Harness's displeasure, '. . . I am rather afraid my captain (Vibart) is something of a schemer. He is to begin with a married man (generally a scheming lot); then he has a convenient ailment, gout, by which he can generally command sick leave . . .' [1]

Curling continues:

This is the best inn without exception I have ever seen in South Africa in this town: the dinners are capital and so well served. Wine and beer is (sic), of course expensive. Beer 1d a glass, claret (dinner) 10/- a bottle and champagne £1 but dinner is only 3/- and breakfast and lunch, 2/-. Some of our fellows have had their baggage sent up from Maritzburg. They find it all ruined, most of it is broken and all mildewed and moth-eaten. Mine, I have not opened for nearly two years and I quite expect to find it entirely ruined. I shall sell anything that remains before I leave the country. I fear much now that I shall be sent to India about next March with the King's Dragoon Guards and shall arrive just in time for the hot weather. If ever I get to England again, they may get me out again if they can. I am afraid you will not know me when next we meet; this life has taken so much out of one.

The Dutchmen are threatening to fight and here a large force of troops are collected. There I believe it will end in smoke.

12ᵗʰ December 1879 Pretoria To Mama

No letters have arrived for more than a month. I know how letters go astray out here and so don't feel uncomfortable about it but it is depressing not hearing from you.

Sir Garnet Wolseley arrived four days ago from Sococcreni's (*Sekukuni*) Country where he has had an easy but successful campaign. I am going to the Chief of Staff about our own affairs tomorrow but it is difficult to know what to ask for. I believe my duty is to ask to be sent at once to join my Battery but should I do so, goodbye to all chances of soon coming home and the only thing to look forward to will be a prolonged living in tents in Afghanistan.

I am rather afraid of my health too and fear I shall not be able to stand a hot climate without proper protection from the sun. If I ask to be sent home on my way to India, it will be very likely be refused and they may not think I have done the right thing to ask to go home when my Battery is in enemy's country.

I am commanding the Battery now and am writing all day long in a tent, anything but pleasant work. I shall be very glad to get away as I don't want to get mixed up in the innumerable muddles that all the different accounts and stores ledgers are in. Col.

Harness is pretty certain to be recalled to put things straight. He should never have been allowed to go away. He has prevented me going and from getting another medal, as now I suppose it will be too late to get one.

I have been down with fever (Common Camp Fever) for four or five days but am all right again now. This place is so intensely hot. At noon, the sun is quite vertical and English tents are no protection. What a fuss they are making about all the Zulu soldiers. Many of them that we read about as having been feted, did nothing at all.

Curling expresses his frustration at having been saddled with sorting out the Battery's accounts which had been left in a muddle by the departure of the reluctant Captain Vibart. Colonel Law also seems to have been instrumental in blocking Curling's transfer, thus making him ineligible for another coveted campaign medal. In the event, fighting again flared up in Afghanistan and Henry Curling did receive an Afghan War campaign medal.

There was some justification for resenting the reception that homecoming soldiers were receiving in England. Curling and his Battery had served in South Africa for almost two years and there was a sense that they had been forgotten and not been included in the Nation's outpouring of gratitude.

Finally, Henry Curling received his marching orders and departed for Durban. From here he wrote what was to be a poignant letter, as a tragedy was about to visit the Curling family:

25th January 1880 Pinetown, Natal To Mama

I don't know how to thank you for your thoughtfulness in writing both to Bombay and Natal. I am quite ashamed that you should take the thankless task of writing duplicate letters. If you know the pleasure they give me I think you would be pleased. I trust Lizzie's illness is not so serious as you fear: I have delayed writing to Willy to congratulate him until I hear a more favourable account. Your last letter is dated 12th December and your next which should arrive tomorrow will, I hope, as it has invariably done since I left England, bring good news.

How delighted Papa must be at having a grandson. I was hoping it would be a boy.

I looked forward for the last year to spending part of the year in the South of France with you but it is not to be. You seem glad that I am not as I ought to be in Cabul now commanding a battery as I ought to have been. I should have had a nearly certain chance of a brevet. This war will, I suppose, last another six months: it will give me another medal but will prevent my taking any steps to get away on leave or by exchanging. The Indian reliefs seem to be done at present in such a haphazard way that it is quite impossible to tell which batteries come home or go abroad.

My battery has been abroad since 1866, as long as any in the country yet. I see by the papers that batteries are coming home that have been out a far shorter time. I intend to get home as soon as possible: this life is terrible, no comforts, bad food and constant rough work tells on one very much. Except for the last month, I have never sat at a table with a tablecloth. Even now you never see such a thing as a napkin and the food we get would disgrace any lodging house in England. Our common drink has been spirits and dirty water, except when we could get beer at 5s a bottle and Champagne at £1 a bottle which was not often.

Of course nothing matters when you are actually campaigning but two years of this kind of life are enough to make me look forward with horror to a continuance of it.

The climate of the coast where we now are is tropical: pineapples are cultivated in the fields and there are sugar plantations about a mile off. It is always hot and we miss the cool nights we got up country. I am living in a house, which is better than a tent, but the houses out here are for the most part built entirely of tin (*galvanised iron*) and don't keep out the heat. My bedroom is 9 feet square and much resembles the cabin of a ship. The attendance in the hotel is of a most shadowy description: there is but one white maid who waits at table, does the rooms and everything but the cooking, which is done by a cooly in their usual greasy way. The inn is kept by a common man who was a labourer once and his wife who formerly was a cook but who is far too fine a lady now to do anything. They and their little children dine and take all their meals with us. However, any change is pleasant after camp life. Today is the 25<sup>th</sup> and by the 4<sup>th</sup> of next month, we hope to be steaming towards India. The 4<sup>th</sup> Regt. that is going on the *Malabar* has arrived here and we only await the troopship which is to take us to Bombay.

There is a rumour that Sir Garnet Wolseley and his staff accompany us to India. It seems difficult to believe it as it means superceding the Commander-in-Chief in India. It will put us to much discomfort but will have the advantage that I shall have an opportunity of making the General's acquaintance.

How very flat the storming of Socooeni's (sic) town has fallen in England. Sir Garnet thought he had made a great coup. Are the Conservative's going out? Should they do so, we shall soon have a general peace: I think everybody is tired of these continual little wars and their expense. This letter will be forwarded to you at Cannes. It seems useless for me to try and write direct to you though when I am in India it is quite on the line of post as I suppose they would take the letter out at Marseilles if it was directed direct to you. We had the thermometer indoors yesterday up to 110 deg, the highest I have ever seen it since I have been out here. Today, in consequence, it is raining and comparatively cool.

Curling's final letter contains the tragic news of Lizzie's death following the birth of a son.[2] In it, he comes close to expressing his regret in choosing a military career with its enforced bachelorhood instead of the comforts of a domestic life:

31<sup>st</sup> January 1880 Pinetown To Mama

I was terribly shocked by your last letter with its sad news. I did not think from your previous letter that there was much danger. Poor Willy; I am quite ashamed at having grumbled about the little ills that one must always expect to meet in life while you have had this terrible sorrow. Although I have not seen Lizzie for several years I seem to know her quite well: she wrote me such kind sisterly letters that one felt that she was quite one of us.

Her last letter was written only the day before her confinement and was as usual as cheery and happy as could be. Willy must feel his life quite changed; they seemed to be everything to each other. I have always envied him his house and could not help constantly comparing his happy state with the homeless life I am living now. We never know what is best for us I suppose.

I hardly like to write to Willy. One can say nothing that will not bring up painful thoughts after two months have softened a little of his grief.

The *Malabar* is expected tomorrow: we embark the day following should she arrive punctually which is doubtful.

The Mail is due on Tuesday so I hope to get another letter from you before starting. The English mail leaves tomorrow so this will be your last from me until I arrive in Bombay unless we are delayed which is never improbable.

I think now that I am going to India it is hardly worthwhile to continue to send the *Pall Mall Budget*. It arrives only occasionally and seldom until it is a week behind the other papers. In India I believe there is no difficulty in seeing all the papers. Please continue to send the local paper: it is very welcome and seldom fails to arrive.

I hope you are having a pleasant time at Cannes and got over the journey without being knocked up. Give my love to Papa and Willy should he be with you . . .

Curling did, finally, embark on the *Malabar* on 4 February and sailed for Bombay. From there he travelled north, through the Punjab and the Khyber Pass until he reached the Afghan capital, Kabul. Here he took up his appointment as a Captain with C/3 Battery at the British cantonment.

The Third Afghan War did not end until that September with General Robert's epic 300 mile march from Kabul to lift the siege of Kandahar. Curling's Battery stayed behind at Kabul, as the more portable Mountain Batteries were favoured and better suited to the rugged terrain. Curling remained at Kabul for six months before the British, both unable and reluctant to occupy both the capital and Kandahar, withdrew to hold the strategic Kurram Valley and the Khyber Pass on the North West Frontier. Finally, Henry Curling returned home in early 1881, having served abroad without leave for three years.

The rest of his career was peaceful, uneventful and unspectacular. On 6 February 1885, he was promoted to Major and given command of D/3 Battery at Aldershot and Exeter. It was regarded as an exceptionally smart field battery so that for some years it was selected as the instructional battery at Okehampton Camp.

In 1895, Curling, now a lieutenant colonel, was made Commanding Officer of the Royal Artillery in Egypt. He was there at the time when Kitchener was appointed Sirdar and planned the invasion of the Sudan and the belated revenge for the killing of Gordon of Khartoum. Curling's fighting days were over, however, for he was transferred to command the Garrison Artillery at Dover, just a short distance from his Ramsgate home. A final appointment, which took him to Pembroke Dock, saw him retire as a full Colonel on 16 April 1902.

A lifelong bachelor, he lived out the rest of his life at the family home, Chylton Lodge, Ramsgate. Comfortably off, he retained his interest in his old corps that had been his home for over thirty years. He generously gave donations to his former Battery and helped old comrades. In 1903, he followed both his father and brother by becoming a Justice of the Peace and, whenever he was in Ramsgate, he frequently sat on the bench. Like his parents, he had developed a liking for the French Riviera and spent much of his time in Menton.

When his brother, Willy, died Curling remained close to his nephew, Graham, as well as his sisters, Mary and Emily. On New Year's Day, 1910, Henry Curling passed away at Chylton Lodge, aged sixty-three. After a service held at the Holy Trinity Church, he was buried at the Ramsgate Cemetery alongside his parents.[3]

One thing Curling would not do during his retirement was to talk about his Zulu War experiences and it must have surprised many who read his obituary to learn that he had been at Isandlwana. Indeed, his obituary in the local *East Kent Times* made only passing mention of his military career and none about his miraculous escape. Instead, it was left to an old comrade to write a fulsome obituary in the *Royal Artillery Leaflet*, to reveal Henry Curling's part in the greatest British military disaster.

Henry Curling was not a great military figure but, by virtue of his escape from the front line at Isandlwana, he was unique. The few survivors of the battle were either interviewed or recorded their experiences in articles and books. Curling, apart from his statement to the Court of Enquiry, chose to remain silent about Isandlwana for the rest of his life. Apart from his natural reticence, perhaps there were deeper psychological reasons for this reluctance to talk about this episode of his life.

It is now recognized that many survivors experience feelings of guilt for having survived while their companions perished. Curling may have wondered why he had lived and Captain Smith, a popular and talented officer, died. Colonel Harness, who deeply mourned Smith's death, may have inadvertently conveyed this impression to Curling. Certainly he was not overly sympathetic towards his subaltern and may have subconsciously resented Curling's survival.

Another reason may have been that the experience was just too terrible to recall and that it was best to be pushed into the background. It would be wrong, however, to give the impression that Curling was a tortured soul for he was, by all accounts, a quiet and calm man, at peace with himself. He lived out his life as a well-liked and respected man, generous with his wealth and time. It is typical of the man that, even in death, he wished to remain anonymous for even his grave bears no reference to his life, merely noting his age and date of his death.[4] If it were not for the preservation of his letters by the family, his life, and in particular his role in the Zulu War, would have been long forgotten and gone forever.

Notes

1   *Invasion of Zululand* by Sonia Clark, Brenthurst Press, 1979, p. 176.
2   Elizabeth Ann Curling died on 17 December 1879, at the age of twenty-five, giving birth to William Graham. Willy later remarried to a cousin, Amelia Morrison Gilmore.
3   *East Kent Times*, 2 January 1910.
4   Henry Curling's grave is situated on the outer right side of Ramsgate Cemetery. Unfortunately, the white marble cross has either fallen or been pushed over, and now lies on the overgrown bed of the grave.

# Index of Personalities